ONE GOOD WORD MAKES ALL THE DIFFERENCE

BY

ROSE MCCORMICK BRANDON

Magnolia Press

Verses marked AMP are taken from the Amplified Bible, copyright 1965 Zondervan Publishing House.

Verses marked The Message are taken from The Message by Eugene H.

Peterson, copyright 2002 NavPress.

Verses marked NIV are taken from the New International Version, copyright 1984 by The International Bible Society.

One Good Word Makes All the Difference

ISBN 978-0-9780622-4-8

Printed in Canada

Waterloo University, Waterloo, Ontario

THANKS . . .

In my mid-twenties, I thought I was destined to remain single. Then my cousin Corrine set me up on a blind date with a friend of her then boyfriend. That date turned out to be a perfect match for me.

To Doug, who has always encouraged and supported my desire to write, with all my love, forever.

To our children, Melody, Carson and Peter – you gave me the three most exciting days of my life. After the excitement died down, you made me laugh, lose sleep and worry more than I thought possible. You taught your father and me that we really could love someone enough to lay down our lives for them.

To my mother, Mildred McCormick, who always has been, and still is, an inspiration and role model.

To my Savior, Jesus Christ, who took my going-nowhere life and made it purposeful.

Rose McCormick Brandon

CONTENTS

A Good Word at the Right Time

Words spoken at the right time are like gold apples in a silver setting. Proverbs 25:11

After the birth of my first child, Melody, while still in hospital, I fell into a weepy gloom, which made no sense. My child was healthy and beautiful. Her wide blue eyes, glowing skin and rounded cheeks presented a prettier picture than any air-brushed magazine baby. It seemed too amazing that she was mine.

So why the tears? Was it because I'd barely slept since arriving at the maternity ward forty-eight hours earlier? Was sleeplessness to blame for the paranoid thoughts that circled my brain?

Besides insomnia and paranoia, for the first time in my life I lost my appetite. Food tasted like sawdust. It was all I could do to swallow a few bites. In all the books I'd read to prepare for motherhood, none had mentioned postpartum depression, or if they did, I'd dismissed it. I'd heard of the *baby blues* but had no idea what the term meant.

My symptoms easily went unnoticed. No one knew I lay in bed awake at night or that I was turning away food. And those thoughts that seemed sane when they first bounced into mind and disconcertingly weird after contemplation – no one found out about them. They were invisible.

One symptom of post-partum depression was visible – my tears. For days, tear ducts ran like taps turning my eyes into red rings. One afternoon, lying on my hospital bed, sun shining in the window, my baby asleep in a plastic bassinette beside me, I wiped at my face and blew my nose. A nurse rushing down the hallway suddenly turned into my room. She strode over and stood between me and the window. "I notice you're crying a lot," she said.

I nodded, unable to speak because a lump constricted my throat. She laid her hand on my arm and in a kind voice said, "It's not unusual for new mothers to cry. Those feelings won't last forever. Give yourself time." According to her, the blues would gradually lift and I would feel well again.

In the photos my husband took of me holding our baby before our little family left the hospital, my eyes matched my pink top. At home, I continued to drag my sleep-deprived body around. More than once, I found myself dreaming while awake. Food remained tasteless. Strange thoughts still pinged back and forth in my brain. I held onto the nurse's encouraging words - my condition was temporary. That meant the symptoms would diminish.

After four months, I was able to lie down in the afternoon while Melody napped and sleep solidly for two to three hours. Rest eased my brain fog. I began to enjoy daily walks, pushing the stroller up and down neighbourhood streets. A few happy hours here and there turned into a general feeling of wellbeing. And my appetite returned. (Loss of appetite was the only symptom of post-partum depression that I hoped would be permanent.)

Hanging onto the nurse's kind words helped me recover. She gave me hope for the future and that's what I needed to cope with my present circumstances.

Words, spoken and written, can impart encouragement, hope and comfort. Good words, passed from one person to another, have power to help and heal. I don't remember the nurse's face, or her name, but her words found a home in my heart for a lifetime.

As you read this book, I pray my words will find a home in your heart, that they will encourage, comfort and help to restore you.

Consider how precious you are to the Lord,

Not a mere speck of God-formed humanity on the planet,

Much more than that –

You are His treasure, highly valued and cherished.

God's Business is Encouragement

Barnabas was a man known as the Son of Encouragement.
The early church sent Barnabas to Antioch to encourage.

Barnabas went to Tarsus to look for Saul.

He brought Saul to Antioch.

Barnabas urged everyone to continue in the grace of God.

(Acts 4:36, 9:27, 11:22, 25, 26, 13:43)

Barnabas was busy spreading encouragement.

The world needs a Barnabas army, people on a mission to encourage others.

On an Encouraging Note

We strengthen one another with words . . .

I'd carried a heavy heart for weeks. Work in a social services office kept my mind occupied during the day. In the mornings I stuffed my anxious thoughts into a file cabinet at the back of my mind and locked it. I'll open those files and examine them later, I told myself. At work, other people's problems required space in my head. They needed warmth, a smile, concern from me.

By quitting time, my shoulders ached from leaning against my drawer of troubles to keep it shut. When I slipped in the side door of our home and mounted the three steps into my kitchen, a dark cloud of discouragement pressed against me. The drawer flew open. Its contents thudded into my chest, lodged there, a tangled lump of misery. At the moment I passed the dining room table, after-work tears stung my eyes.

A square envelope lay on my placemat. Tiny letters revealed the name of the sender – Valerie Feighen. For years, our paths had crossed. Our last connection had been at a women's retreat in Michigan where we were guests, she as musician, I as speaker. We'd had a heart-to-heart while hiking along the waterfront and through the resort's mapled forest. Val's passionate faith inspired meaningful conversation. Each encounter with her left me with a stronger confidence in God and in my role as one of His servants. A few months earlier, I'd picked up the phone on my work desk to hear Val's excited voice say, "I just read your article in the paper and I want to tell you to keep on doing what you're doing. You're blessing God and everyone who reads your work." A short conversation, she didn't want to disturb me at work she said. Her words made my tired eyes lift from the clutter of my desk. I caught a glimpse of God's story weaving itself into my life, my words, my work.

Our locations and schedules kept me from regular contact with Val. I'd shared my present heartache with a few close friends but I hadn't thought to call Val. A prayer specialist, she would've invoked heaven on my behalf . . . if I'd called.

I sat at the table, slid a finger under the sealed flap and pulled out a card. Red and white roses encircled the words: *I hold you in my heart.* Inside I read, *"As I sat before the Lord this morning your face came before my eyes and I felt an urge to pray for you. I did. You are precious to the Lord and He holds you close to His heart. Remember, He will never leave you nor forsake you as you are going through this difficulty. You are in the palm of His mighty hand."*

Val's words fell into my soul like rain into parched crevices. I pressed the note to my heart and cherished it as a personal message from God to me. He cared. Cared enough to whisper my name to Val . . . not only whisper my name but reveal my need . . . a need she could not have known through any other source.

The note's message ended with *"God be with you as you are going through this difficult time."* I did believe God was with me but I hadn't felt Him with me until I opened Val's card. The next day I wrote a letter of thanks for her encouraging words. My soul had found a partner who sensed the depth of my need and responded. "I can't tell you how much it means to know that you're praying for me," I wrote.

During that particular challenge, I read Val's note often. In time, the situation that had caused my suffering improved. Today, it's almost forgotten. But Val's note isn't forgotten. It's posted on the bulletin board above my desk where it reminds me of the value of words, especially encouraging words.

—-◆— — —◆— — —◆— — —◆— — —◆— — —◆— — —◆— — —◆— — —◆— — —◆— — —◆—-

When this story was first published, I sent a copy of it, with a note, to Val Feighen. She responded - "your words couldn't have come at a better time." She had been feeling useless, with no significant role to play in God's mission. (Even people who have made encouraging others a life habit suffer from discouragement. They too need encouraging words.) Reading this story confirmed to Val that though she may not know the outcome of her encouraging words, it was important for her to continue on her God-given mission of encouragement.

A Song for the Discouraged

For months, I've been praying earnestly for a breakthrough in a certain matter. Several times it looked like the answer had arrived then the bottom would fell out again. Yesterday, discouragement took hold of me. What's the use in praying anyway, I thought. How long will this situation go on? Why aren't you listening Lord? These depressing questions swirled in my mind.

I told the Lord I was worn-out from praying, sick of waiting for answers. This morning my regular reading took me to Psalm 126 in the Message.

And now, God, do it again – Bring rains to

our drought-stricken lives

So those who planted their crops in despair

Will shout hurrahs at the harvest,

So those who went off with heavy hearts

Will come home laughing, with armloads of blessing.

Eugene Peterson comments on this passage: "It's clear that the one who wrote this psalm and those who sang it were no strangers to the dark side of things." These folks knew about tears and suffering.

Everyone suffers. But only God knows how to turn our tears into joy. The people who sang this psalm went out with heavy hearts like mine but returned home laughing, blessed. Today, this scripture nourished my soul, that part of me that nothing can reach but God's Spirit.

Jesus expressed this nourishing of the soul when he told his worried disciples that he had food to eat that they hadn't yet experienced. This scripture made my heart joyful again and caused me to look beyond my discouragement. It helped me to experience joy in the midst of my suffering. It also gave me perspective – what a small suffering mine is compared to that of the psalm's writer.

My faith renewed, I'm praying – *Yes God, do it again, rain down on my prayer crops, fill my arms with harvest blessings.*

Weak in Christ

We are weak in Him yet by God's power we shall live.
2 Corinthians 13:4

I was guest speaker at a women's retreat on the weekend. During my three days there I sensed the Holy Spirit ministering through me. Though finding time for rest was difficult, I didn't feel tired while there. But when I trudged through the front door of my home Sunday evening, I felt the weight of household duties rise to meet me. Tiredness pressed into my bones.

When my body's fatigued or in pain, my mind doesn't function well. Even reading a book takes more concentration than I can muster. When weakness overtakes me, I'm keenly aware of my fragile humanness.

Jesus-followers often use the phrase "strong in the Lord." Because Sister Jones' faith is unshaken by many challenges we say she's strong in the Lord. We also use this to describe people who do what we consider great things for God. Most believers from time to time do great things for God. But I don't plan to do anything great today. Today I'd describe myself as *weak in the Lord*, and I'm finding it a pleasant place. My weakness reminds me how dependant on Him I really am. I'm not self-sufficient, far from it. Feeling my humanity is good for me.

Today I crawl under God's wing. He lowers it over me. I snuggle into Him; rest my head on His strong shoulder. Tomorrow I might wake up ready to take on the world again, maybe, but today I plan to fully experience weakness because I am, after all, only human.

"Keep me as the apple of your eye; hide me under the shadow of your wing." Psalm 17:8 NIV

Interruption

An interesting word that's often the means of bringing encouragement to others.

I discovered the true meaning of the word interruption – a personally designed encounter from God to make his ways known.

Rebecca Barlow Jordan

Divine Interruptions

It happened on a winter Monday, my day off. Carson was eating breakfast before getting dressed and running off to high school. I poured a cup of tea and joined him at the table, thankful for a gentle start. My tea was still warm when a knock came at the door. A neighbour wanted to borrow a snow shovel. Daisy, our disobedient English Bull Terrier, bounded up from the family room to greet him. As he bent to ruffle her ears, she glimpsed daylight between his legs and shoved her bulky body through the opening and dashed out the door. I shouted, "Daisy, come!" in my best authoritarian voice. She hoisted her elegant (some say homely) nose and continued down the driveway toward the street.

Our neighbour apologized and quickly retreated to his snow removal task. He lives near enough to know we've had more than a few Daisy chases. Carson jumped from his cereal bowl and threw on his clothing. The two of us climbed into the van to search the snow-piled streets for a dog we loved in spite of her wicked streak. We circled the subdivision several times, scanned driveways and backyards, asked men pushing snow blowers, "Have you seen a brindle coloured dog, long nose, short hair?" After forty-five minutes driving up and down streets, we spotted her snout protruding from between two five-foot snow banks. We stopped, opened the van's sliding door and motioned for her to get in. She hesitated, reluctant to end her adventure. Carson scooped her onto the back seat where she shivered all the way home.

The doggie pursuit changed our plans. Carson was late for school and my morning wasn't the quiet one I relished on my days off. A hundred and fifty years before Daisy interrupted my plans, Annie Keary wrote, "One can feel that perhaps one's true work - one's work for God, consists in doing some trifling haphazard thing that has been thrown into one's day. It is not a waste of time, as one is tempted to think, it is the most important part of the work of the day - the part one can best offer to God."[1]

Chasing a rebellious dog shouldn't be viewed as a waste of time but my true work for God? I searched for the good in this divine interruption and discovered these positives.

During the search, I was tempted to express my frustration "That's it. This is my last chase. Daisy has to go." My relationship with Daisy was a love-hate one; Carson's was love only. If his patience held without complaining, so should mine. He has many life interruptions yet to face. It's important he sees me handling mine without griping. The doggy-chase gave me an opportunity to demonstrate patience even if I had to dig deep to find it.

Keary's thought that a detour from one's plans could be the most important part of the day caused me to wonder why Daisy challenged my patience on a Monday morning. Could it be God's way of testing Sunday's worship? Anyone can warm a church pew. To carry lessons learned from the pew into the following week seems to be my eternal challenge. In the end, I fared not too badly in the Monday doggy chase.

Many significant events in Jesus' ministry began as interruptions – a sick woman touched his garment, a synagogue leader begged him to heal his daughter, a funeral procession, a stoning – Jesus turned each interruption into one of the "good works I have shown you from my Father" (John 10:32) There's a God-lesson in every experience, even an unwelcome interruption.

Interruptions still frustrate me. But I'm trying to see God in them, revealing Himself in the casual, mundane, disagreeable, petty events of my ordinary days. Flat tires, balking cars, snowstorms, late planes, overloaded buses, crammed waiting rooms, crashing computers, unwelcome phone calls - even mutinous mutts – all these can weave their threads into our plans and become our true work for God.

(1) Daily Strength for Daily Needs, compiled by Mary Wilder Tileston 1891 (available as free download)

Monday at the Church

The smallest act of giving or receiving makes you a true apprentice. You won't lose out on a thing. Matthew 10:43 (The Message)

The car moaned. A few tries later its reluctant motor kicked in. I drove the ten minute trip to my job in our church office, not long enough for the engine to warm. My fingers were still numb as I turned the key in the door. Soon the ancient furnace forced radiators to beat out a tinny rhythm.

Icy winds attacked the building's steep roof. Howls droned from the sanctuary's pinnacled ceiling. A sheet of ice snapped free from the roof and fell to the ground, cracking the frosty air like a gun. Its fearsome sound froze my fingers in mid-air over my keyboard.

School had been cancelled, a snow day declared. My three children were enjoying a cozy day at home with Dad. I grumbled inwardly about having to work. Suddenly, a rush of cold air drifted through my office door, under the desk and attacked my feet. Someone had opened the front door. When I looked, a boy of nine or ten stood in the lobby, red, bare hands cupped over his ears.

"Can I use the bathroom?" he asked.

"Follow me and I'll show you where it is," I said. On our way downstairs, I found out he lived next door and had never been inside the church. He had a "so this is what it looks like in here" expression on his face.

While my young guest was in the men's room, I remembered that an elderly lady in the church had knitted several sets of mitts and hats for a northern mission. She brought them in too late to be included in the shipment. When my young visitor returned, I offered him a set in a multi-striped masculine design.

Smiling, he stepped forward and let me cover his hands and head in woolly warmth. When the new mittens were tucked under his jacket sleeves and his ears covered, he reached up and gave me a I-really-like-you-lady hug.

"It's no accident you came here today," I told him. "God knew I had a warm hat and a pair of mitts and He wanted you to have them."

Ready to brave the cold again, he gave a cheerful wave and clunked outside in his floppy boots. As I returned to my office, I think I heard God whisper, "Isn't this the best place for you to be today?"

Lord, thank you for bringing this small stranger to my door. His coming reminded me that my purpose is always to do whatever good I can.

Listening

If we listen we'll hear encouraging words

Extreme busyness, whether at school, kirk or market, is a symptom of deficient vitality . . . it is no good speaking to such folk: they cannot be idle; their nature is not generous enough.

Robert Louis Stevenson

The Period: A Productive Pause

At ten, our youngest son Peter complained about a church group leader who talked too much. I encouraged him to be tolerant by pointing out that some people simply talk more than others.

Peter said, "But no one else gets a chance to say anything."

"You need to be patient and wait for your turn to speak," I told him. "But Mom, he talks way too much. Everybody else has a period sitting on their tongue but Mr. Jones doesn't."

Aahhh, the period. That small dot at the end of sentences that brings the reader to a full stop. In conversation, periods are invisible but still necessary. We indicate them with pauses designed to allow others the chance to speak. In Mark Twain's humorous tale, Roughing It, the main character travels across country by stage coach. On one leg of his journey, he meets a fellow traveler unacquainted with the conversational period. Lamenting his misfortune, he writes, "The fountains of her great deep were opened up, and she rained the nine parts of speech, forty days and forty nights, metaphorically speaking, and buried us under a desolating deluge of trivial gossip." [1]

Not all marathon talkers match the biblical status Twain attributes to his fictional babbler. Still, I was once forced to flee when the distant strains of a well-known marathon-talker drifted through the aisles of a grocery store. That hideous sound pumped enough adrenalin through my veins to send me scurrying through the aisles collecting groceries at top speed. I peeked around corners before wheeling my buggy into the next section, fearful that at any moment the source of the voice might appear. At the check-out with two strangers behind me, I sighed with relief. I'd make it to the car without being assaulted by this skillful chatterer.

Windy wonders love the conversation circle. They suck in more than their share of oxygen. Their prey, light-headed and weak, search for excuses to escape. "My goodness, I just remembered I'm supposed to pick up Billy after swim practice."

Keys in hand, they rush for the door. No chatterbox has been indicted for murder. So far. But, that doesn't mean that words, when they come by the ton, don't kill. How many speeches die when the main point is suffocated beneath an avalanche of unnecessary words? Potentially interesting discussions are slain by word terrorists who hi-jack conversations and steer them into monologue country, the graveyard of meaningful exchange.

Anyone can get over losing the core point of a sermon. But often the real victim of too much talking and not enough listening is friendship. Friendship is a loss that isn't easily recovered. Bonds develop between people who understand the value of the conversational pause. During pauses, we learn about others, their experiences, loves, talents, their style, heartbreaks and joys. People connect with us when we listen. The simple act of listening builds strong bonds between people.

Peter was right. Everyone should have a period sitting on their tongues.

(1) Mark Twain, Roughing It, New York City: Airmont Publishing Company, Inc. 1967

Listening Prayer

*The pause is not only important in conversation
but in prayer.*

Jesus taught the spare use of words: "When you pray, do not keep on babbling like pagans, for they think they will be heard because of their many words" (Matthew 6:7 NIV). We can find the heart-to-heart relationship we crave with God if we intentionally listen. Andrew Murray, who wrote much on prayer, admits it may be difficult to learn quietness but he writes, "the little season will bring a peace and a rest that give blessing not only in prayer but all the day." [1]

Holy moments often occur in stillness. Don, an anonymous contributor to Philip Yancey's book, Prayer, tells of a visit to a dying friend in the hospital. After Don and the friend took communion together, the sick man told Don that an angel had visited his bedside the previous day with this message – *you will soon be going to heaven.* Both men felt enveloped in a holy moment that demanded silence. After several minutes, Don spoke in tongues for the first time, an experience he described as profound.

Good things happen during periodic pauses, with God and with people.

(1) Andrew Murray, Waiting on God, Chicago: Moody Press

Make the Call

The thought was there when I awoke. Even after school lunches were packed, breakfast served and three kids kissed out the door, it lodged my mind like a stone. I sipped coffee, read a book and tried to ignore it but the weight of it increased.

"Phone Janice," the thought urged. I cleared the table and loaded the dishwasher instead. The thought persisted.

Several weeks earlier Janice had joined a Bible class I attended. Her fearful eyes, seldom making direct contact, announced to me and to others that she felt worthless and wary. I introduced myself, praying silently for Jesus to show me how to befriend her. Janice's wooden response gave me the impression she wished I'd go away. Each week, after our Bible study, I approached her. It was hard work finding something to talk about. I kept trying because I sensed God leading me to be her friend but she didn't seem to be warming up to me.   In my kitchen that morning, I resisted the urge to call Janice. Another one-sided conversation didn't appeal to me. Finally, thinking the thought must be from God, I looked up her number and dialed. When Janice answered, I began with, "I was thinking about you today and thought I'd call and see how you are." I'd never called before but she didn't seem surprised to hear from me. Her voice sounded warmer than usual. The rest of the conversation was unmemorable. It lasted no more than five minutes.

A few days later, Janice surprised me by dropping by with a fresh batch of chocolate chip cookies. She stood at my door with the tray, her eyes meeting mine and a smile twitching nervously at the corners of her mouth. I invited her in. During our visit, I discovered she loved to read. I sent her home with a stack of books, most of them personal stories written by men and women who had experienced amazing transformations in their lives.

She read all the books and returned them in a couple of weeks. I gave her more. This continued for months. To keep our exchange going, I had to visit my local Christian book store often. Our friendship blossomed. She kept bringing cookies and I kept sharing books. I wanted to give her a Bible but thought she might think that was too pushy.

One day, she said, "There was a prayer in one of those books you gave me. I thought it couldn't do me any harm so I prayed it."

"What kind of prayer was it?"

"Something about giving your life to Jesus."

That's all she wanted to say about the prayer. A few days later, I bought her a paper back Bible and told her, "This is yours to keep. You don't have to return it." She stuffed it into the backpack she always carried. I wondered if it would be read.

During our visits over the following year, she told me about her horrifying childhood and expanded her baking to include the best bread my family had ever tasted. One day, she pulled the Bible out of her backpack to show me she'd been reading it. A giant elastic band held its creased cover and loose pages together.

I opened it and saw large portions underlined and whole sections highlighted. Hundreds of tiny notations crept around the margins. Some pages had little white space left.

"I'm so proud of you." It was all I could say. She welcomed a hug once in a while so I gave her one.

Half-way out the door she turned back and said, "The cookies and bread are the only way I know to say thank you."

"For what?" I wondered.

"Do you remember the first time you called me?"   I said I did.

"That day I had decided to kill myself but I wanted to give God one more chance. I told Him that if you phoned me, I'd know I shouldn't do it."

Her words took my breath away. I hadn't guessed how important my phone call had been. In the years since, Janice has faced many difficult challenges but she's still following Jesus.

Selah

One of the first things I do when I get to the cottage is remove my watch. The minute I walk through the door, time becomes unimportant. We eat when we're hungry, read till we fall asleep. We sit on the deck and listen to the birds with an early (or not so early) cup of coffee. The orderliness of time is imbedded in creation. Seven days of 24 hours make a week, four weeks form a 28-day cycle of the moon circling the earth. Hearts beat, harvests ripen, babies are birthed in harmony with God's rhythm. Work is necessary. It pays the mortgage, clothes the kids and puts food on the table. It can also dominate. When it does, we miss God's rhythm of rest. The cadence of our lives must include pauses. The soul craves time to think, relax, explore, to stare at the sky and get lost in its beauty, to listen to earth's sounds and consider how many generations have listened to those same sounds.

One word appears many times in the Psalms – Selah. It means to *pause and calmly ponder these things.* The psalmist David uses it at the end of profound statements. For example, Psalm 24:10 reads, "Who is this King of glory? The Lord of hosts, He is the King of glory. Selah." This word tells the reader to stop, think and take in the rich meaning of this statement. This holy intermission, Selah, allows truth to sink deep into our minds and souls. Is your life lacking Selah? Ask God to show you how to include pauses in your day. Enter into His rhythm of rest and experience the difference it makes in your level of joy.

Prayer Pause -
Father, I long to thoughtfully consider Your Word, Your gift of salvation, Your creation. Help me to pause and calmly think of You.

Listening to My Hair Grow

Learn to live in God's rest. In the calmness of spirit it will give, your soul will reflect, as in a mirror, the beauty of the Lord and the tumult of men's lives will be calmed in your presence, as your tumults have been calmed in His presence.
Hannah Whitall Smith [1]

I found myself tangled in a web of connections linking me to too many responsibilities. A husband with his own full schedule, three children with homework, after-school lessons and maturing personalities, plus cleaning, laundry, appointments, leadership of a women's organization, speaking engagements – an endless to-do list controlled my life.

My job in a church office filled the few remaining slots in my overcrowded mind. My job description didn't include working Sundays but legitimate needs seemed to tug at me from the moment I entered the church doors. I smiled on the outside but gritted my teeth on the inside.

The only sparkle left in my eyes came from pent-up tears. Knots upset my stomach and migraine headaches ruined at least one day out of every week. I didn't need a doctor to tell me I was overwhelmed. Robert Louis Stevenson wrote of the person I was becoming – *Extreme busyness, whether at school, kirk or market, is a symptom of deficient vitality . . . It is no good speaking to such folk: they cannot be idle; their nature is not generous enough.* [2]

At the end of my strength, a summer sabbatical sounded like a solution.

I arranged for the church to hire a student to fill my job for the summer. Doug and I bought a trailer on St. Joseph's Island, an hour's drive from our home in Sault Ste. Marie. We moved, all five of us, into our twenty-five foot summer home. There were three bunk-beds on an upper platform at the back of the trailer, one for each child. And a kitchen table that miraculously became a double bed for Doug and me.

One day a friend dropped by to visit. "I couldn't bear to sit here all summer and listen to my hair grow," she said. Listening to my hair grow was exactly what I needed. My tanned kids fished with their dad, swam till they wrinkled, built cities in the sand, rode bikes on dirt roads, collected toads and pudding stones (a rock unique to the area) and played Battleship and Scrabble on rainy days. Often they fell asleep at our nightly campfire and had to be carried to bed. Each morning they awoke within a stretched arm of one another.

No television, no traffic, no telephone, no calendar. I read my Bible and other books while chickadees sang and chipmunks scurried. Every day I biked to the general store for the daily paper, our connection to the outside world. When it was open, I visited the local library where I rediscovered Agatha Christie. I haven't let her get too far away since.

My summer sabbatical gave me time to reflect on the person I'd become - a worrier with mixed-up priorities, pleasing everyone but the people who mattered most, my husband and children. And a hurrier with no time for interruptions. At some point in my busyness, I'd lost my Mary ways and become an anxious Martha. (These sisters were good friends to Jesus. You can read their story in Luke 10.) That summer, I delighted in the colors and sounds of creation, let the wind and rain mess my hair, swam in the bay and walked country roads.

I spent hours on my lounger - at the beach, by the camp fire, sometimes even napping, and refused to feel an ounce of guilt for my idleness. Even my friend's comment about doing nothing but listening to my hair grow didn't upset me. At one time I would have felt obligated to prove I wasn't a slacker. Sleep came easily at night and I had no dread of morning.

I read my Bible with a listening heart. I became quiet enough to hear God urging me to write. A new thought came to me while staring into the camp fire - if I organized the world in a mountain of file folders, planned extraordinary meetings, showed off the smartest, best-behaved, best-dressed children and decorated my home like a pro but didn't follow God's promptings, what would it all benefit me?

Labor Day arrived too soon. A lump lodged in my throat when we packed our belongings and closed the door to our cramped summer home that could be cleaned in fifteen minutes. That fall, I requested that my work week be reduced to four days instead of five. Less money for a better quality of life. Gradually, I learned to say *no* to responsibilities that weren't mine and to save my energy for the ones that were. Changing my pleaser personality is a lifetime project but that first summer at the trailer put me on the right track.

My summer sabbaticals at the trailer continued for five years. It was there that I learned to love the sound of my hair growing.

(1) Marie Henry, Hannah Whitall Smith, Minneapolis, Minnesota, Bethany House Publishers 1984
(2) Robert Louise Stevenson, Essays of Robert Louis Stevenson, Biblio Bazaar 2006

Everyone has a story to tell.

A word here, a word there, and before you know it, a whole story is written.

Tell how your story connects with God's story because His big story is what makes our small stories significant.

Out on a Limb

An 84 year-old woman went skydiving to celebrate her birthday. Another octogenarian bungee jumped off a bridge to mark his 85th . These two defied gravity and the ancient voices of their mothers telling them that just because all their friends were foolish enough to jump off bridges, doesn't mean they should do the same. They did it to satisfy their youthful desire for adventure. People, who defy their fears and survive to do a follow-up interview, report these experiences as thrilling and liberating. But risk-taking isn't limited to physical adventure.

One of my acts of bravery began when an article outlined itself in my brain. I had a resume of only two published credits, one in my Bible college yearbook and the other in a writing contest. I put the piece to paper and mailed it to the editor of my denomination's magazine. After dropping the submission in the mailbox, I tortured myself with images of the editor exclaiming, "I've never read such rubbish!" A few weeks later, a letter arrived from this editor saying he intended to publish my work. "Do send more articles on any subject," he added. My writer's heart did a joyful leap. I hadn't parachuted from a tall building onto a trampoline but I'd crawled out on a tiny limb of possibility and – gasp – it had held.

By casting my words on uncertain waters, I'd risked rejection, a thread no one wants to weave into the fabric of their lives. The alternative was to suppress the desire to write, a desire that felt like it came from God. But I wasn't 100% positive. I had to knock on the publishing door to find out. Fear of rejection can make us dumb when we should speak and glue our feet to the floor when we should move forward. This fear whispers negative comments like - you'll make a fool of yourself, surely others more talented, more connected and more prepared than you should write these articles. If I'd heeded these messages, I would still be filling my desk drawer with un-submitted articles.

The need for security is rooted deeply in human nature. We see its influence in the way some responded to Jesus' call to follow Him. They marveled at His words, recognized His divine authority but when know-it-all Pharisees accused them of being swept off their feet with lies and threatened them with excommunication, they distanced themselves from Jesus (John 7:4553). When we step out of our comfort zones, criticism will come, and often from unexpected places. People may misunderstand our motives. They may not see value in our goals or they may simply not get us. It's alright to shed a few tears over rejection because it's painful but it's not alright to let a strong need for security dictate whether we follow God's will for our lives.

The other basic need rooted in our natures is for significance, a sense that our contribution to the big picture matters. Significance doesn't mean becoming famous. It doesn't mean we're the best at what we do; it simply means we feel better about ourselves when we step forward and offer our contribution. Taking risks for worthy reasons adds exhilaration to life and that increases our sense of significance.

Many God-called people let God-given ideas lie dormant because they fear failure or rejection. God is writing a story in each person's life. Our pages hum with joy, grief, pain and pleasure but no novel is complete without adventure. The adventure chapters in our stories chronicle the times we've chosen significance over security, the times we've knocked on strangers' doors, uncertain whether we'd arrived at the right address. For many submitting an article to an editor who may reject it isn't risky – for me it was and sometimes still is.

I haven't sky-dived or bungee-jumped but I suspect taking the plunge helps people face challenges in other areas of life. The bottom line for Christ-followers is this: if we don't risk following wherever He leads, we'll never know the joy of crawling out on a limb and finding ourselves exactly where He wants us to be.

Believe in Your Story

Give yourself permission to believe in the validity and the power of your own story. I am a professional member of an organization of writers who are Christian, The Word Guild. Each year hundreds of us enter work published during the previous twelve months, vying for awards in several categories of fiction and non-fiction books and articles. I started entering three years ago. The first year my work was shortlisted but didn't place. The next year I placed first in personal experience and second in another category.

Last year, I entered two of my published articles. I thought both were good, very good in fact, so you can imagine my surprise when I didn't even shortlist. At first I felt miffed. Something must be wrong with the judges. Yes, for sure, it had to be their problem, it couldn't be mine.

After the awards gala, I received, as is the organization's custom, copies of the pieces I had entered with comments from the judges. Two articles. Different judges. Almost identical comments. This is the gist of their critique: This writer knows how to tell a story. (Thumbs up.) Then each went on to say how disappointed they were when my personal essay descended into stories and quotes from *experts*. "I wanted to hear what you had to say," one judge wrote. Another judge commented that I'd begun well, hooked the reader then lost the reader when I gave my voice to "experts" who weren't nearly as interesting. (I did that because I didn't really believe in my words.)

I remembered my previous shortlisted and winning essays. I'd written from my heart, opened a window for the reader to see into my soul. Somewhere between year two and year three, I'd decided my views needed confirmation from others. I know how this happened. I wrote a few articles for a magazine that sculpted my outlines. They suggested who to interview. I followed their advice. I had to or my work wouldn't have made it to the publishing stage.

Some subjects require confirmation from experts but I'd carried this practice into my personal experience essays - a mistake.

Each writer comes to the task of writing with her own life experiences. Those experiences shape the writer's point of view. I can quote other writers, and I still do, but I'm careful now not to give my voice to someone else. The writer's voice is his greatest asset.

You may not be a writer but you still have a story to tell. Your story is shaped by your people, your surroundings and your experiences. Tell your story from your heart as simply as you can. Especially tell how your story connects with God's story because His big story is what makes our small stories significant.

Life is a Poem

If you build your life on my words, said Jesus, you will be like a house built on a rock. When rains pour and rivers flood, your house won't collapse. (My paraphrase of Matthew 7:24)

The Greek word Jesus used for the idea of building a life on His word is poiema. The English word poem comes from this word. Poets use words in creative ways to build something original.

"Be a poet," Jesus is saying. "Take my words and build a life with them." His words build solid foundations. His words can also decorate our lives and turn them into something beautiful.

I met a pretty mother of two small children. She told how she'd been addicted to heroin, sold her body on the downtown streets and lived in constant rage. I looked into her clear eyes and soft face. I couldn't imagine her slashing her arms and screaming like an animal but one rainy night, in the grizzly downtown core, she went berserk. She felt like she was in hell she said.

She'd built her life on a sand bar. A hurricane had rushed in from the sea and flattened it. In the middle of her torment she remembered that God loved her. On that ugly night this young woman began to build a meaningful life, a poem, because, as Corrie ten Boom often said, "No darkness is so deep that Jesus is not deeper still."

It's never too late for God to take the meaningless jumble of our lives and turn them into a beautiful poem.

"One well-chosen word at a time. One stanza of service at a time. And with our words and deeds, we can leave something beautiful behind in the lives of others." Eugene H. Peterson.

H i s Word . . . .

We have words but
He is The Living Word
Long after our words have
vanished His will remain. . . .

Many have pronounced the death sentence on His Word
Yet the Bible remains the best-selling book on the planet.

A Gift for All Occasions

A copy of Scripture, wherever it's placed, is never wasted. Years ago, my husband Doug found the Bible I had stashed in the glove compartment of my car. Like a prospector mining for gold, he uncovered treasures in a book he hadn't read since Sunday School days.

When Doug reached the Gospel of John, he found the real Treasure: "Then Jesus cried out, 'Whoever believes in me does not believe in me only, but in the one who sent me" (John 12:44, NIV). Doug bowed his head and prayed, "I've always believed in you God, now I believe in your Son Jesus too."

Giving a Bible to someone can be the most effective method of guiding them to Christ. There are several reasons why.

Giving scripture is sowing seed. A Bible is like a packet of seeds waiting to be planted. The book won't accomplish anything sitting on a shelf but when it's opened and read, the words take root and grow in the good soil of a welcoming heart.

The gift of a Bible fits any occasion. A few years ago, Doug and I attended a birthday bash for one of his co-workers. It was a golden opportunity to place a Bible in his hands. Our friend, not yet a believer, has mentioned several times how much he appreciated our gift.

Scripture has its own voice. Its words are always appropriate, its witness always effective.

In a parable Jesus likened a farmer who sows seed in a field to sowing the seed of His Word in people's hearts (Matthew 13). When we scatter the seed of God's Word, it grows and blossoms, sometimes in unlikely places.

Love Your Bible Enough to Wear it Out

Everyone has them – a pair of scruffy shoes that should be thrown away. Mine sit on a shelf at the back door – an ancient pair of black loafers. Miles of wear have molded them to the shape my feet. When I slip into them, my toes sink into hollows on the inner sole. I always intend to change into garden clogs before wading into my perennial bed but I seldom do. Now, horizontal grooves from weeding on bended knees wave across the insteps of these dilapidated shoes.

With its frayed stitching and floppy cover, my favorite Bible resembles my leather loafers. Coffee stains dot its pages but the burgundy coloured Amplified version fits me as comfortably as my old shoes. Not long ago, I treated myself to a classy looking new black covered Bible in the New International Version. I carried it to church and Bible studies and tried to love it. But gradually I reverted to the rumpled Amplified. Scribbled notes wander across its margins. Dates, stars, names and arrows draw my attention to verses that have special meaning. I love its wordiness. Others may find the bracketed alternate meanings an interruption but I find myself wishing for more explanation.

A bible should become as personal as well-worn sneakers. Once a new Christian picked up my bible from our coffee table – at that time I used a leather-bound Schofield KJV study Bible with my name embossed in gold on the cover. I'd owned it for several years and it showed. "You write in your Bible?" she said.

"Yes. If a verse touches my heart or teaches me something, I underline it. And sometimes I make notes beside it."

She spent several hours that afternoon underlining my special passages in her fresh bible. "You're going to end up with a bible that's more mine than yours," I told her. She wanted it to look used she said. And I get that. Nothing is as sad as a seldom-read Bible. More than just another religious book, a copy of scripture contains sacred words that penetrate the deepest recesses of the human soul. No other writing, no matter how stirring and brilliant achieves this.

Like comfortable shabby shoes, a loved Bible travels. And not only to religious events. It visits park benches, cafes, laundromats, airports, trains, buses and fast-food places. It's not afraid of greasy fingers or breakfast crumbs. It doesn't cringe when a baby reaches out, as one of mine did, and rips a page from Romans. I taped the tattered leaf in place and now its stiffness draws my attention to what many consider the greatest stand-alone book of all sixty-six. Men like William Tyndale sacrificed their lives to put a copy of scripture in common hands like mine. Since then, many have believed in Jesus through no other witness but the Bible. My husband Doug is one of them. When we were dating he found the Bible (the leather-bound KJV) I had stashed in the glove compartment of my car during my wanderings from God. Beginning in Genesis, he read every day for months. One day, when he had reached the New Testament, he prayed, "God, I not only believe in you but now I believe in your son Jesus."

David van Biema, Religion Editor for Time Magazine, wrote – "The Bible is the most influential book ever written. Not only is it the best selling book of all time, it is the best selling book of the year every year."[1] Today's robust bible sales must have Voltaire red-faced in his grave. He predicted that fifty years after his death there would not be a single Bible remaining on earth. The sad reality is that a large percentage of bibles lie on shelves and night stands, their pages unruffled by human fingers and free of ink spots.

Helen, a woman who attends our church, found one of those neglected bibles at a time when she was lonely, depressed and contemplating suicide. Alone in her apartment, she read for hours each day. At night she placed the Bible under her pillow as she slept. "I found my Lord in this book," she said pointing to a hard cover volume held together with ribbon. "He saved my life and I have dedicated myself fully to Him." Helen is now wearing out her second bible.

As a fifth grader, my friend Patricia Capy, received a Gideon New Testament. She read it from cover to cover and still follows the practice of reading the Bible as a complete book. She's lost track of how many times she's read it through. It's so familiar to her that when searching for a passage, she often knows its exact location on the page. That happens when we become as comfortable with our Bibles as we are in an old pair of shoes.

[1] David van Brema   The Case for Teaching the Bible   Time Magazine   April 8, 2007

Three Little Words

Sometimes a small dose of good medicine is all that's needed,

Most days, I read 1-3 chapters of the Bible. But some days, I don't get beyond a few words. Today I read, *"Abide in me."* (John 15:4)These three little power-packed words stopped me in my tracks. I've been busy with many projects – a house to pack up for a big move, articles to write, goodbyes, visits, new phones and address changes. I'm also planning messages for an upcoming retreat. Al l good activities, all necessary but they draw me into a whirlwind. My thoughts scan a never-ending to-do list. I'm desperate to scribble checkmarks beside each job to show I've completed it.

Abide in me. Those words drew me away from necessities and back to the essential – my relationship with God.

Abide means to live. I can make myself at home in God. In all my present activities, I can find rest, perhaps not for my body but for my inner self, the part of me that generates the most unrest.

Rest comes best to me when I pause to consider the marvels of creation. The structure of a simple leaf, the grooves in the rocks I collected for my garden, flowers that bloom in ditches – beauty everywhere, beauty that calls out – abide in me.

The Creator of all this invites us to breathe deeply in Him. This is the secret to enjoying God.

Today, let these three little words, *Abide in Me,* draw you into God's joy.

OH! God

A walk through the Bible left me awestruck in Job

In January I resolved to read through the Bible. My journey began well. I cruised through several chapters each day, visited many strong characters on route – Abraham, Joseph, Moses, Joshua. Naomi, a bitter woman turned sweet, grabbed my attention. As she rocked an unexpected grandson on her knee, I waded into Samuel, Kings and Chronicles, Esther, and finally, Job. I'd heard enough depressing sermons from this book to last a life-time. Its forty-two chapters loomed like a haunted, forbidding forest.

Spring had arrived. On sunny days, I read by the river or in the backyard. Job's dreary story seemed out of sync with buds and birds. So I detoured around it and went straight to the Psalms. It wasn't long before I reached Isaiah. What a prophet, and what a writer. Isaiah's beautiful word pictures encourage and comfort the reader. By summer, I'd reached Malachi, the end of the Old Testament. I congratulated myself. Only 27 books to go and I'd be finished.

How can you feel good about reading the Bible through if you skip Job? That niggling question interrupted my back-patting. I'd placed a mental tick *beside* each book as I'd completed it. No tick beside Job.

Seeking shade from the sun, I moved my lawn chair under a maple tree. My fingers leafed through the pages of a worn Amplified version of the Bible. "There was a man in the land of Uz whose name was Job. . ." with that my mind left the heat of the back yard and dove into the dark cold waters of Job. At the outset Satan seeks God's consent to test Job's faith. Permission granted. Nobody relays this information to Job, an injustice, in my view. Before the end of the first chapter invaders have stolen his livestock, killed his servants and Job's ten children have died in a hurricane. Satan, upset by Job's positive response to his calamities, asks God for permission to afflict Job's health. He gets the go-ahead. The poor man's body breaks out in boils from head to toe. Grief has angered his wife; she turns on him. By this time, Job's neighbours are crossing the street to avoid meeting him.

As if his troubles weren't stacked high enough, Job's long-winded self-righteous friends arrive to console him. These three "wise men" badger troubled Job to confess his sins and renounce pride. Their platitude-ridden speeches exasperate him. ". . . wearisome and miserable comforters are you all! Will your futile words of wind have no end? Or what makes you so bold to answer [me like this]? I also could speak as you do, if you were in my stead; I could join words together against you and shake my head at you" (Job 16:1-3 AMP). Job's rebuke insults his comforters. They retaliate by predicting more suffering for their beloved friend. I'm aching for Job and weary of his friends and their endless conversation. My journey slows. Anything that blooms, moves or speaks distracts me from reading.

By mid-August Job concludes his three friends are hypocrites. Whew! Without a lawyer to represent him, he defends himself and swears he's innocent of breaking God's laws. Then a fourth, younger friend, Elihu, takes five chapters to defend God. The engine of my Bible reading sputtered uphill – until the first chill of fall began turning the leaves of my maple golden. That's when I reached chapter 38 and discovered I wasn't the only one fed up with the philosophizing of Job and his tedious friends.

God's seizes Job (and the reader) by the collar. He forces our noses to the ground to consider whose hands laid earth's foundation. Then with Superman flash, he circles the constellations and asks, "Can you bind the chains of Pleiades?" Breathless Job stutters – "I am of small account and vile!" then clasps his hand over his mouth. But his spiritual awakening isn't finished. The Lord plunges Job to ocean depths and challenges him to take on the sea monster. He declines. The grand finale, another question, "So you're afraid to awaken a crocodile but not afraid to thumb your nose at me, the beast's creator?" Remorseful Job recognizes his sin and confesses. I do too. I'd forgotten, or perhaps never had grasped, what A. W. Tozer calls the OH! of God. "When God Himself appears before the mind, awesome, vast and incomprehensible, then the mind sinks into silence and the heart cries out O Lord God!"[1] Call it reverence, the fear of God, or awe, discovering God's OH! is glimpsing His incomprehensible power in a way that reveals our true feeble state. OH! immobilizes. It quakes the joints and dizzies the mind.

I'd jogged through the last five chapters of Job, lost track of time in wonderment. As the cover closed, I felt a sadness that comes with saying goodbye to a loved character in a novel. Before moving on, I promised to return often, to keep God's OH! aflame in my heart.

(1) A. W. Tozer, Born After Midnight, Christian Publications Inc., Pennsylvania

NO – a helpful word

I've learned to say no to many things in order to say yes to the

main thing.

Selwyn Hughes

The Main Thing

While busy with church-based activities, I felt God calling me to open my home and invite my neighbors to a Bible study. Saying yes to this, led to leadership in an international Christian women's organization that lasted for a decade. The work involved speaking, traveling and teaching. God gave me energy, time and the devotion needed to do the work. But, I often felt torn between this outside-the-church work and my involvements inside the church. My three children deserved most of my energy and the left-over portion had to be dealt out wisely. The general teaching was that, after family, the church had first dibs on a parishioner's time. I didn't question the truth of this teaching. Instead, I struggled to meet my family's needs while keeping up with church responsibilities and following my passion in women's ministries. For a while, I managed it. Things became complicated as my children grew. They became involved in activities – sports, music, church, socials – and these had to be worked into my schedule. For many years, I pursued *excellence*, a recurring theme in books and sermons.

Eventually over-commitment got the best of me. When alone, which wasn't often enough for my personality type, I became weepy. For no reason that I could identify, I struggled with anger. Responsibilities overwhelmed me. I felt like an unwise runner who had used up all her energy in the first few kilometers of the race and had no strength left to reach the finish line.

Jesus said, "You're blessed when you're at the end of your rope. With less of you there is more of God and his rule."(The Message)

With my fingers barely clinging to the end of my rope, I felt forced to ask the question, "What is wrong with me?" These are my answers.

I was a people-pleaser. What would the pastor and others in my church think of me if I admitted I was exhausted and needed to quit the choir and stop teaching Sunday School? I had to admit that I cared too much about what they thought.

I was proud of my work. Yes, I did put my heart into it but I was also proud in an unhealthy way. Could someone else take my place and do a better job? Yes. That answer felt wrong because it knocked me off my pedestal but it also felt right because it relieved me of being the only one who could do the job.

I had church confused with God. Because my primary ministry was with a para-church organization, I felt obligated to give my church as much time as I gave my primary calling. I had misunderstood my obligations and that caused me to involve myself in too many causes.

I was depriving my family. When I didn't work outside the home I was able to spend quality time to my family. My return to work added another demanding dimension to my life. It became impossible for me to divide my time between family, ministry and church. There just wasn't enough of it.

I was in a weak place – physically, emotionally and spiritually. I felt fearful of the future if I continued down the same path. I made deep cuts in my church calendar, some in women's ministry and none with my family. This was only the beginning. I still tended to over-commit my time and continued to have difficulty saying no, especially to opportunities that appealed to me. Another decision helped. If the commitment was temporary, like a six-week class or a one-time speaking engagement, I'd give myself permission to say yes. As my involvements diminished, I felt stirred to write, something I'd dabbled in but never found the time to pursue. Gradually, writing became my main thing.

As for the local church, I think more wisdom should be shown when employing volunteer service from young mothers. When their initial enthusiasm turns sour, they're reluctant to step inside the church's doors for fear someone will ask them to provide free babysitting, a pan of lasagna, ten dozen cookies, to lend a hand with clean-up, or a dozen other things.

God wants us to think and pray about our main work. Whatever that is, we must devote ourselves to it. That means saying NO to every request that steals time from the main thing. Besides our primary calling, two things remain constant in importance: good family relationships and friendships with people who add to our lives.

Prayer of Response:

Lord, help me to become quiet enough to hear from you about the main focus of my life. Let my thoughts drift in you and find joy in the miracles that surround me. As I prune excess from my life, I lean on your wisdom for guidance.

It's Okay to Say No, Even in Church

Many sermons manage to relay the subtle (sometimes not so subtle) message that the people in the pew simply aren't doing enough and anyone who is doing enough isn't doing it well enough. These types of sermons make people feel guilty about such things as the amount of money they give, their level of church participation and their faithfulness to church attendance.

One preacher often used this refrain: if you love the pastor, you'll attend church Sunday mornings; if you love the people, you'll also attend Sunday night services but if you love the Lord you'll be here on Wednesday nights for Bible study too. A few titters came from the congregation each time he said this. I don't think it's funny at all. These kinds of smug assertions discourage people. The real message it sends is this: if you're not here every time the doors are open, you'd better feel guilty about it.

Many people arrive at church in need of encouragement. Their hearts long for God's Word and the kindness and love of fellow believers. They're overwhelmed by home and job responsibilities and in need of a peaceful atmosphere of worship. They long for an anointed sermon, for heartfelt prayer. Parishioners aren't encouraged by a razzamatazz of announcements that add to the weight of their crowded calendars. People don't come to church to hear that ten pans of lasagna and a hundred dozen cookies are needed for the following week. Or that a busload of teens is descending on the church and every one of them will require a billet. And no one - man, woman or child - needs to hear a drawn-out plea for money. All these are fine in small doses but many churches don't know how to measure small doses.

What sincere church-goers need is affection and thoughtfulness from other members of the congregation. Sadly, many come and go without receiving these simple things.

I know, I know, somebody has to do the heavy lifting in church. The question each person in the pew needs to answer is –

does it need to be me? After years of exhausting "service to the Lord," I finally gave myself permission to say NO to many church requests – and it was one of the best things I've done. It freed me to think about what Jesus wants me to do with my life - surely there's more to my service for God than writing my name on endless miles of sign-up sheets.

Paul wrote in I Corinthians 7:23 (Amplified Version) - "You were bought with a price - purchased with a preciousness and paid for (by Christ); then do not yield yourselves up to become (in your own estimation) slaves to men, (but consider yourself slaves to Christ).

God sees us as individuals, not as just another church member. We each have a calling from God and we've received gifts from Him to fulfill those callings. When the busyness of doing church hinders our calling in Christ; when we feel more discouraged exiting church than entering, something is wrong. And no one can fix it but us.

The best way to start the fixing process is by saying NO to things that hinder and YES to fulfilling God's call in our lives.

Forgiveness – a holy expression

Repentance for the forgiveness of sins will
be preached in His name to all nations . . .

Luke 24:47 (NIV)

Forgiving Miss White

The moment I laid eyes on Miss White I suspected I'd made a mistake. After graduation from Eastern Pentecostal Bible College in Peterborough, Ontario, I accepted an invitation to assist the female pastor of a church in an isolated fishing village on the east coast of Newfoundland. After a flight from Toronto to Gander, I traveled hours by car over rugged but stunning rocky terrain.

On arrival, I expected a cheerful welcome from the middle-aged woman I would live and minister with. Miss White stood on the stoop, arms crossed, eyeing me. It wasn't a welcome-to-the-end-of-the-world smile she offered me but a well-look-what-they've-sent-me this time look.

We settled into three cramped rooms tacked onto the rear of a clapboarded, ocean-front church. Noting the arrival of a newcomer, an Atlantic fog drifted into the bay and smothered the village. Continuous drizzle kinked my hair. At Sunday services, Miss White pumped an ancient accordion and sang with gusto hymns I knew well but her renditions made them almost unrecognizable. The congregation consisted of a half-dozen women with young children, one sixty-something bachelor and two or three senior couples, sturdy people all, accustomed to hardship. And to Miss White's hymns. From the first service, I became known to all as "the girl from the mainland," a title that separated me from them in a way I, as a young woman alone in a strange place, found heartbreaking.

Miss White ruled in the church and in our mist-covered parsonage. No first names allowed even in private conversation. "If you call me Nellie, and I call you Rose, then Miss McCormick, it'd only be a matter of time before you slipped and called me Nellie in front of the church members." That slippery slope would lead to parishioners calling us by our first names – a huge sign of disrespect.

No wearing of pants permitted. And jeans? Dear God, wasn't the devil's hand in the making of those? No make-up. "If the barn needs painting, I say paint it. But this barn," Miss White ran her fingers over her wrinkled cheeks, "needs no paint." *In my opinion, Miss White, every barn looks better with a fresh coat of paint.* That's what I wanted to say.

No visiting parishioners alone. "We goes together or we don't go at all." The appearance of unity was Miss White's top priority. We took turns cooking but the menu was hers. We cleaned, studied, prayed and slept on her schedule. The manse had two bedrooms but "no need for you to have your own room. You can share mine. Saves on the heat bill."

For the first time, I experienced true homesickness. This ailment should be listed in medical journals. It muddled my mind, ruined my appetite and stole my smile. I longed for sunny days and the fresh smells of home. My tears mingled with the depressing fog that refused to lift. I berated myself for naively believing that a seldom-seen corner of my home country wouldn't feel as foreign to me as Mongolia. I longed for time alone to shed my tears and sob out my sadness but Miss White was ever-present. And God seemed distant.

I didn't confide my misery to family back home because private phone conversations were impossible. But I expressed my loneliness in a letter to Carolyn MacVichie, a college roommate from the mainland who was teaching in Gander. We'd been friends since age fourteen. One weekend she drove to visit me at the end of the world. We talked for hours about people and places we both knew. We cruised around the area like young girls should and visited a few historic sites. I laughed with her. Before Carolyn made our driveway vacant again, she laid her hand on my shoulder and prayed out loud for me.

After Carolyn's departure, Miss White, lips pursed, said "You should've invited me to go with you two when you went for a drive." *I was trying to get away from you.*

"I'm a fun-loving person. Everybody always says I'm youngish looking for my age."

Would you like to know what I think?

Christmas neared. I used what little money I had saved to fly home. Before leaving, I packed my belongings in boxes and shoved them under the bed. *If I don't come back, it'll be easier for Nellie to send my things.*

After two weeks with normal people in familiar surroundings, I decided not to return to Newfoundland. I phoned Miss White and asked her to send my things. She tried to talk me into returning. "It won't look good, Miss McCormick, if you don't come back."

It won't look good for you, you mean. "Sorry, Miss White, I've made other plans."

Four months of fog, drizzle and isolation was endurable; four months with Miss White wasn't.

That desolate church on the edge of the Atlantic would've become a short scene in my history but Miss White kept reappearing. She wrote letters. In some she apologized for not understanding me. *It's a little late for apologies.* She sent trinkets as peace offerings. I tore up the letters, despising even the sight of her handwriting, and dumped every gift in the garbage. I sent no return letters, no thank you cards, nothing.

I moved to a new city, got a job in a downtown office and found a church. But by then I'd started to sour on church. I found fault in everything from their dress styles to the way services were conducted. I stashed my well-worn Bible in the glove compartment of my blue Datsun and, except for an occasional visit, quit church. New friendships with co-workers meant that I spent more time in their worlds and less in mine. Miss White's letters stopped.

About five years after I left Miss White, three important people crossed my path, my future husband and two co-workers. Because of them, my faith revived, not instantly but gradually over a two-year period. One day while reading John 10, I saw myself as the stray lamb, the one rescued by the Good Shepherd and brought back to the flock. Thankfulness welled in my soul. And then, for no reason at all, I thought of Miss White for the first time in years.

Unlike other thoughts of her, this one wasn't repugnant. Instead of hatred, I felt affection for her.

That day, I wrote to Miss White. In my letter, I mentioned God's kindness to me and asked her to forgive me for the hatred I'd felt toward her. When that letter dropped into the mailbox at the corner of our street, a literal weight lifted from my shoulders.

Miss White wrote back – "I enquired about you and knew you had drifted away from God. I felt so responsible. I'm overjoyed to hear that all is well between us." Miss White and I corresponded for many years. Her letters, no longer torn up, but treasured, became symbols of the holy work of forgiveness God did in me.

Note:

I can't take credit for forgiving Miss White (not her real name). My only action was to respond to God's invitation to receive forgiveness for my own sins. When I did, He planted love in my heart for her. Forgiveness doesn't roll off the tongue; it comes from the heart. Saying "I forgive you," doesn't make it so. Only God gives us the ability to forgive. But if we are willing to "get rid of all bitterness, rage and anger and forgive others as Christ forgave us" (Ephesians 4:31,32), we can experience spiritual freedom. That freedom allowed me to forgive Miss White.

Forgiveness, a Gift You Give Yourself

My friend and long-time prayer partner, Enis Chamberlain, arrived at the Toronto airport early for her flight to London. She piled *her* bags on a cart and headed to a coffee shop for lunch. A woman came up behind her and asked for directions. A kind person, Enis tried to help. During the exchange her handbag was snatched from the cart. Her passport, credit cards, cash, everything she needed for her vacation was stolen.

Authorities explained that she'd been played. When she turned to look at the woman asking for help, an accomplice to the crime had stolen her purse. Enis was devastated. Several phone calls later, helpful airline staff had her on the plane. "Don't let this ruin your plans. Go and enjoy yourself," her husband said. But as she settled into her seat on the plane, a knot of despair lodged in her chest. How could I be so stupid? Why didn't I have my purse looped over my shoulder? I must look naive, that's why these thieves picked on me. This is the story of my life, always getting picked on. Ugly, self-accusing thoughts rolled through her mind.

She leaned back on the headrest. "God, help me," she prayed. A thought, quiet but firm, came into her mind - you need to forgive yourself. She prayed again, "I do Lord, I do forgive myself. I recognize that anyone can be taken advantage of." Immediately, the self-accusing thoughts stopped and her shame vanished.

A stolen purse may rank low on the list of things we need to forgive ourselves for but the despair Enis felt wasn't much different than the despair we feel over bigger issues. She hadn't sinned; a sin was committed against her. Often it isn't sin that causes us to accuse ourselves but our own perceived failures, unwise decisions, missed opportunities, lack of confidence, unsophisticated social skills and dozens of other weaknesses we may imagine in ourselves.

An important step toward forgiving ourselves is acceptance. We can work on our weaknesses and emphasize our strengths but we can't change our personalities. Years ago, I read a few books on the four basic temperaments. I found these helpful but not as much as when I later discovered the more refined Myers-Briggs personality analysis. Results pegged me as a true introvert. This fact alone settled many anxieties for me. Understanding our temperament helps us develop a healthy self-respect. It also gives us an appreciation for other personalities.

Too many Christians spend too much energy trying to live someone else's life. "I've tried to be quiet and gentle," my friend Mary Luchetti said, "but it's just not me. I couldn't keep it up." As a new Christian, she had looked around the church and concluded that the best Christians were the quiet, gentle ones. She tried on a few "godly" personalities before she realized that God had changed her from a sinner into a saint but He hadn't transformed her into a completely different personality.

One of my other good friends, Darlene Wilson, a devoted Christian for many years, said, "I've tried to be someone other than me as far back as I can remember, thinking maybe if I was like so and so, I'd be a better me. The other day, I told God I haven't got the energy to do it any longer. That's when He told me he liked the real me." Darlene describes this as her personal epiphany. It was a holy, life-changing moment for her. God-moments like Darlene's produce inner changes that free people to develop deep, personal relationships with Him.

Replicating someone else's personality is not only dishonest but exhausting.

Another obstacle stands in the way of self-forgiveness. It's revealed in a question sent to me by a reader of my blog. She asked, "Why do we hold ourselves to a higher standard than we hold others?" We accept major flaws in others but we deride ourselves for minor infractions. Why? There are no easy answers. A personality with a strong tendency toward perfectionism, being firstborn in a large family, taking responsibilities at a young age and pride are all possible answers. God helps each person find the answer to this question for themselves.

Another possible answer is that harsh preaching causes sensitive believers to imagine God's disapproval. Most people possess an enormous capacity to make themselves miserable without any help from judgmental, condemning sermons. God enjoys His creation. He takes pleasure in all of it but especially in the people who are redeemed by the sacrificed life of His own precious Son. He delights in us, imperfections and all. The Holy Spirit convicts us of sin but once that sin is confessed there's no further condemnation. We're loved (and liked) by a God who rejoices over us and doesn't accuse us (Zephaniah 3:17). We serve a kind Lord, One aware of our frailties and full of compassion.

When, after having her purse stolen, Enis prayed for the ability to forgive herself, she received immediate release from self-accusing thoughts.

God helps us, not only to forgive others, but ourselves.

A Prayer of Response:

Lord, I recognize that I'm not superhuman. I've made mistakes that have made me angry with myself. I want to be free from self-accusing thoughts. Today I forgive myself for _____ (name the act).

Those who enter into Christ no longer have to live under a black cloud. A new power is in operation. The Spirit of life in Christ, like a strong wind, has magnificently cleared the air, freeing you from a fated lifetime of brutal tyranny at the hands of sin and death. (Romans 8:1,2 - The Message)

Faithfulness – a forever word

I will sing of the mercies of the LORD for ever: with my mouth will I make known thy faithfulness to all generations.

Psalm 89:1 (KJV)

Faithful to the Prodigal

The prodigal phase of my life began soon after I graduated from Bible College. Unable to find my niche, I drifted away from God. With my once keen interest in the Bible and Christian service in decline, I became enamored by the cool, more glamorous lifestyles my friends at work enjoyed.

My collection of Christian books and Bible commentaries ended up in a trunk, my Bible stuffed into the glove compartment of my car. One by one, traces of my former Christian life disappeared. I still believed in God. If interrogated, I couldn't deny His existence. But, as I saw it, He'd distanced himself for reasons unknown and left me alone to find my way.

Church services became repugnant. When I stopped attending, I felt relieved of a heavy duty. I stayed in touch with some believing friends but kept clear of the "tsk-tsk what a shame she used to be such a fine Christian" crowd. Five years passed. Then, in the space of one year, three people came into my life. First, I met my husband Doug. He knew little about my Christian past and I planned to keep it that way. But some time between our engagement and wedding, he discovered the Bible I'd stashed in the glove compartment and started reading it every day on his lunch hour.

While Doug became increasingly excited about the Bible, I made a new friend at work, Grace Fenton. By then, I was working at Westinghouse in Hamilton. Like me, Grace had turned her back on God and the church. Strangely, this fact bonded us. One day, Grace surprised me by saying she really wanted to get back to church. As a two-time divorcee she felt unwelcome in the denomination where her father had been a prominent pastor.

"I need you to take me to your church," she said.

I didn't consider myself to have a church but Grace's friendship meant a lot to me. I agreed to accompany her to the church I'd last attended, People's Church in Hamilton. With its large congregation, it would be easy to slip in and out unnoticed. Doug, who hadn't been to a church service since childhood, came with us.

I intended it as one-time event but Doug and Grace were drawn to the warm personal style of worship. Grace described a feeling of something good happening to her.

After that, we showed up whenever we had a free Sunday. Doug continued his Bible reading and soon after, committed his life to Christ. Grace began to call herself a born-again Christian. I felt nervous. My plan to keep God in storage wasn't working.

A new person arrived on the scene. When I transferred to a different division of the company, the office and coffee room was abuzz with gossip about Betty Zelinski. I soon learned that the secretary to the Director of Research, a vivacious party-girl, had become a Christian six months earlier. Her zeal had overflowed into the workplace. Betty seemed not to notice that her coworkers disapproved. Their snide remarks didn't hinder her from telling about her life-transforming experience.

Soon after I arrived, Betty told me she'd been praying that a Christian would be hired to fill my position. Since God had answered every single prayer she'd prayed thus far, she believed I was heaven-sent. I explained to her that I had once been a Christian but had given up my faith. "I'm what you would call a backslider," I said.

Betty replied, "Call yourself whatever you want, I know God sent you." She made me her new best friend.

When it came to the Bible, Betty was on a learning curve. Every day she grilled me for information and I found myself reaching into my locked storage box for information I'd tried to forget. One day, she came to my desk with a brilliant idea.

"When the guys (the engineers we worked with) are out, let's go downstairs to the empty office. I want you to lay hands on me so I can be filled with the Holy Spirit."

I didn't refuse to pray for Betty but found ways to delay. A few weeks later, she was filled with the Spirit in her bedroom at home. My friendship with Betty and Grace and Doug's growing interest in spiritual matters worked together to stir the embers of my faith.

I didn't want to jump back into the faith life or become a churchy person. No public commitments for me. Like Nicodemus, I went to Jesus privately. My faith remained a secret, even from Doug, Grace and Betty, for several months. Then one Sunday morning during a worship service, I heard these words, like a whisper in my soul, several times – *the faithfulness of God*. At that moment I realized that in spite of my unfaithfulness to God, He'd remained faithful to me and had waited respectfully for me to return to Him. He understood my hesitation and nervousness and didn't condemn me for it. In Jesus' story of the prodigal son, the father ran to his son, hugged him and kissed him, before the son asked for forgiveness. The coming of Doug, Grace and Betty was the Father running toward me with open arms. Through them, I saw His faithfulness.

God Runs

One day, an unkempt drifter blistered by the sun, barefoot and bloody staggered into the town center.

At the same time, the CEO of a successful company was sitting at a large desk in front of a massive plate glass window many floors above. He turned and looked down into the town square. He recognized the beggar as his youngest son. The father got up from his desk and ran. As he exited the front doors of his office building at full speed, the father's expensive shoes kicked up dust onto his designer suit.

Two of the CEO's assistants gazed at the scene from their posh offices and one sighed, "The old man's lost his mind."

The other assistant agreed. "He's a fool for that no-good kid of his." He head wagged in disapproval.

The two watched as their boss opened his arms and embraced his rebellious son. He wept on the kid's shoulder and if they'd read his lips correctly, he said, "At last you've come home."

Before the son had uttered a word of regret, the father forgave him for squandering his fortune and living like an idiot. The father forgot the hurtful words the son had hurled at him years before when he'd slammed the door and left home for a better life, cruel words meant to break a parent's heart – *I wish you were dead.*

An assortment of losers, thieves, low-lives, dummies and rebels (just like us) wanted to know what God was like. To answer their curiosity, Jesus told them this story of the loving father. They understood that the rebellious son represented them. For the first time in their lives, they realized the greatness of the Father's love for sinners.

God loves to the point of foolishness. Long after everyone else has given up hope, He watches and yearns for His child's return.

He loves us before we are able to love Him. Look up, God is running toward you.

"God is love." (I John 4:16)

Life Takes us on Detours but God is a Faithful Guide

"The Lord directs the steps of the godly.

He delights in every detail of their lives."

Psalm 37:23 (TLB)

In 2001 tech stock values plummeted. Soon afterward terrorists struck the twin towers in New York City. These two events devastated the financial sector. The previous year my husband's investment business had become successful enough for me to leave my position in a small church office. But before I could ponder what to do with my free time, fall-out from these events threatened our income and I decided to re-enter the workforce.

I checked an on-line job board and found a government-funded organization that needed a part-time information technician. *Able to type a minimum of 75 words per minute* the ad read. In my resume I felt tempted to state - not only can I type more than 75 wpm, I can do it while talking, eating, feeding babies and answering the phone. After tests and interviews I was hired.

That's how I met Ann.

During our second week working together, Ann confided that her son, away at university, had contracted an illness that doctors were unable to diagnose. Through tears she said, "He's so sick he can't attend classes and he's afraid he won't graduate. I worry about him day and night."

"We have a Bible study meeting at our house this week," I told Ann.

"If it's alright with you, I'll mention his name for prayer."

"Your friends don't know me or my son. Do you think they would mind praying for him?"

I assured Ann that we often prayed for people we didn't know. Our small group prayed for Ann's son and soon after he began to show signs of improvement. He continued to gain strength, graduated university and went to teacher's college. His recuperation amazed Ann and she had no qualms about sharing her miracle with our co-workers. Once, as I entered a meeting room, I overheard her say to staff that my prayers had healed her son. I was a bit embarrassed by this but my co-workers didn't smirk. Several said how happy they were for Ann and a few said that they too believed in prayer.

Ann's interest in God increased. She started regularly watching a Christian television program and subscribed to an on-line daily devotional. These contributed to her spiritual development. Ann isn't afraid to tell anyone about her faith in God. Once she confided to me, "I don't know where the words come from. They just flow out of me."

Ann and I often pause from our work to share a brief God moment. One morning during the first week of 2009 she came to my desk and said, "I want you to know that God brought you into my life." I recalled how world events in faraway places had caused my path to intersect with Ann's. As devotional writer, Selwyn Hughes writes," Behind the seemingly chaotic and indiscriminate events of our lives a bigger story, a divine story, is being written."

God often uses world events to up-root and re-plant people. He used the jagged edge of persecution to disperse first century Christians to Judea and Samaria and then to the remotest parts of the earth (Acts 1:8). His goal? To publish His story through the lives of ordinary people.

A year in Auschwitz cruelly unraveled Corrie ten Boom's cozy life. It stole her father, brother, sister, home and her career. From the tattered threads of her previous life, God wove a new purpose that changed her from an unknown fifty-something Dutch watchmaker into a global ambassador for Christ, the author of numerous books and the subject of a biographical movie, The Hiding Place.

Charles Colson, once an advisor to Richard Nixon and a member of the White House in-crowd, warmed himself too close to the flames of Watergate and got burned. He ended up in jail. When Colson gave his life to Christ, heaven's holy fire drove him from politics toward a new purpose – improving life for prisoners.

I see God at work, using tragic circumstances to interrupt my life-path and cause it to intersect with Ann's. The present global financial crisis has the potential to become a major detour on life's highway for many people. It could separate workers from their jobs and families from neighbourhoods, re-adjust retirement plans and interrupt dreams and goals. After shedding a few tears about the altered routes we're forced to take, we need to remember that God often uses detours to lead us to the main road of our lives.

A Moving Experience

He led them by a straight way to a city where they could settle.
Psalm 107:7

Moving was out of the question for many reasons. Our home was located only a block from Doug's office, enabling us to get along with one vehicle. My perennial border in our first backyard showed signs of future glory. Relatives lived nearby. We loved our church and belonged to a closely knit group of young Christian couples.

On the plus side, relocation offered more challenging, potentially rewarding employment for Doug. It also meant he would live in his favorite spot on the planet, at the junction of the Great Lakes. An avid fisherman, he'd spent much time in northern Ontario and he ached to explore more of the north's wilderness and rivers.

"Whither thou goest I will go." Those sounds romantic in a wedding ceremony, but when it came to packing up and actually leaving, they struck me as unfair. So I did what came naturally. I whined. "Why should we move? We've got everything that really matters right here." What I really meant was, "I have everything that matters to me."

"At least be willing to pray about it," my frustrated husband pleaded. Believing God would see things my way, I agreed. A strange thing happened. The more I prayed, the more clearly I saw that relocation wasn't just my husband's idea, it was God's.

The company in Sault Ste. Marie confirmed their job offer with Doug. Our house sold. With a lump in my throat I buckled our two toddlers into their car seats and began the long journey northward.

Doug experienced immediate success in his new job but it meant working long hours. Even with an eleven month-old son and three year-old daughter, my days had many quiet hours during their daytime naps and in the evenings. The phone rarely rang.

Few visitors called and we hadn't bothered to hook up the television. Those alone hours provided time for studying scripture, reading, writing and praying.

Our home stood at the entrance into the subdivision, like a lighthouse in a busy channel. I prayed for the families in our new neighbourhood. One of the first articles I read in the local paper told about the high divorce rate in the city, so I prayed for a reduction in family break-ups. Our next door neighbors had split ten months before and chances of them re-uniting seemed slim. Soon after my prayers began, they got back together. (They never separated again and are still together more than thirty years later.) A few months after the first article, the same newspaper headlined the declining divorce rate in our city. I realize many others were praying too but I took this news as a direct answer to my prayers.

I met Brenda, a young mother in our subdivision, at our new church. We became close friends. I expressed to her my desire to start a women's neighbourhood Bible study. She agreed it was a good idea and wanted to help. We advertised the study in the free section of the newspaper. Within a few months, many women came to my home, some through our ad and others through personal invitation. Most had never attended a Bible study but their hearts were open to God and they had an earnest desire to learn. When our group grew too big for my living room, Brenda opened her home and she taught a study too.

A year later, with the help of many other women in our community, plans were laid to start a chapter of Women's Aglow. Under the umbrella of this ministry, eventually fourteen Bible studies operated in the city. Some of the leaders were young and inexperienced but soon they became capable teachers. A few older godly women came out of retirement to help fill the need for teachers. This network of studies became a blessing to many.

Years after moving from this neighbourhood, I continued to cross paths with people who lived there who became believers.

Though it pained me to leave our first home, the church and friends we loved, I became thankful for this moving experience.

Note: I wrote this when we moved from Hamilton to Sault Ste. Marie. Thirty years later, we moved back to the Hamilton area and back to the same church mentioned in this piece. The following story, Moving Experience Part T|wo, tells of the return story.

Guiding Light (Moving Experience Part Two)

Near the end of a sizzling summer day, my husband Doug and I launched our boat into a nearby bay. We anchored in a narrow strip between two rocky islands where we could count on a cool breeze and a fish or two. Doug let down a wormed line and kept one eye on the fish finder. I lounged, book in hand.

"They're starting to bite!" Doug's rod bent as he reeled an uncooperative pickerel to the surface. I slapped my book down and grabbed the net. With two hands on the handle, I swished under the fish. Doug clipped our catch to a stringer and hung it behind the boat. He baited another hook. I returned to my book. But not for long. "Got another one . . ." Soon our catch reached the allowed number.

Reluctant to leave the lake's refreshing breezes, we took a few fish photos to add to Doug's legendary collection. By the time we tucked our belongings safely into cubbyholes, a reddened sun sat low on the horizon. It painted the clouds pink and streaked the sky purple. Doug checked his watch. "It's later than I realized. We'd better head for shore." In minutes, darkness blanketed the bay. The motor launched us in the direction of the marina, several miles away.

"Shouldn't we go slower at night?" I worried aloud from my first mate's seat. In daylight, boulders jutted above the water's surface. Others hid mere inches below.

"See that beam of light?" Doug pointed to the only green light in a cluster of white ones that shone from trailers and cottages along the shore. "Now look behind us." Two lighthouses cast their beams in our direction. One sat high on a distant rock, the other nearer to us and closer to water level.

"The green light at the marina and the beams from the lighthouses form a straight line. If I align the boat with all three lights, they'll lead us to shore." We motored through night waters and slipped safely into the marina, our trust placed in the wisdom of long-gone seafarers. When it comes to navigating life, no wisdom shines brighter than God's. In September 2008 it was His guiding light that led us through an uncertain time.

All three of our adult children had migrated south. Doug operates his financial business from our home but his head office is in Toronto. For us, relocating from northern Ontario to the southern part of the province made sense. We painted, de-cluttered, made the house sparkle and put it on the market. I emptied closets, unloaded years of sports equipment and swept seldom seen corners of the basement. My heart sang with thoughts of joining my children and living near my little grandson.

Over lunch, one Sunday after church, Doug and I discussed moving plans. I read second thoughts between the lines of his side of the conversation. A lump lodged in my chest. My bags were half-packed, I was ready to wave goodbye. In my mind, the moving van had already backed out of the driveway. Later, alone with God, I prayed, "Please don't let our moving plans fall apart. But . . . (I groaned over that word) if this isn't the right time for us to move, please show me through my job." I worked as a casual employee in the administration office of a large organization. My shifts had dwindled in the past few months. I counted that fact as a check-mark in the pro-moving column. Four days after my reluctant prayer, the office called and offered me full-time employment for an undetermined length of time.

Our moving plans died. Did I cry disappointed tears or praise God for guidance? I did both. Soon after, rumors of an economic collapse shook the financial industry. Investors held a collective breath . . . then a global tsunami, the biggest in our lifetime, emerged from the mysterious dark waters of the money world. It swept away powerbrokers and innocent homeowners alike and left a trail of devastation.

The fall of 2008 produced an unpredictable housing market that made it unwise to buy or sell. We couldn't have chosen a worse time to move Doug's business. My tears over the cancelled move dried up when I realized how much better it was for us to stay put until this economic storm subsided.

We trust mortal ingenuity to guide our boats to shore. How much more can we trust God to guide our lives? Wisdom, as presented in Proverbs, is the art of living skillfully in the earthly conditions in which we find ourselves. It applies to relationships, plans and morals. Solomon wrote, "Listen for God's voice in everything you do, everywhere you go; He's the One who'll keep you on track. (Proverbs 3:6, The Message)."

In the summer of 2010, we finally moved into our southern Ontario home. Our Guide is always faithful . . . in His time.

Prayer - words of holy action.

Talking to God is an amazing privilege. . .

it's astounding that mere humans are allowed to do it.

Prayer Changes Things . . . But Not Everything

When I found myself pregnant with our second child, I prayed that I wouldn't be overdue. During the ten overdue days before our first child, Melody, was born, I became cranky, cumbersome and frustrated.

So sure God agreed with my request and bursting with faith, I told my friends that definitely, absolutely this baby would be born on or before his due date. The due date neared, my mother came to stay with Melody while I was in hospital. (At that time, mothers stayed in hospital for 6 days.)

The due date passed. I became cranky, cumbersome and frustrated. One afternoon while Melody napped, I threw myself on the bed (as much as a nine and a half month pregnant woman can throw herself on a bed) and cried a prayer that went something like this, "Lord, I can't believe you haven't answered my prayer."

An unmistakable inside-my-heart voice answered, ". . . a time to be born."

These few words let me know that no matter how much I prayed, cried and stomped my feet, God had a plan bigger than mine and it included a specific date for my child's birth.

Prayer is a powerful instrument. It does change things . . . but not everything.

The little phrase, a time to be born, comes from a poetic passage in Solomon's book of Ecclesiastes, chapter 3. He lists other realities of life that can't be changed. For example, there's a time to plant and a time to reap.

Eugene Peterson comments on this passage – "there are realities of life that God puts together in His time, not ours."[1] He gives us grace to accept the situations He refuses to change.

I got up from my bed of weeping with a new spring in my step. Ten days past his due date our son Carson entered the world. The lesson I learned while waiting for him has stayed with me – it's right to pray about everything but wrong to insist that God work according to our schedules.

(1) Eugene Peterson, Conversations: The Message, Navpress, Colorado Springs, CO.

Go Forward on Your Knees

The earnest (heartfelt, continued) prayer of a righteous man makes tremendous power available – dynamic in its working. James 5:16 (The Amplified Bible)

Missionaries Jonathan and Rosalind Goforth arrived in China in March 1888. Their assignment to open a new field in the northern section of Honan province was a daunting one. The young couple struggled to learn the language, adjust to the climate and raise a large family in less than desirable surroundings. They met many discouraging challenges, including the death of a child. One day a letter arrived from Hudson Taylor, then a pioneer with China Inland Missions.   He wrote: "We understand North Honan is to be your field; we, as a mission, have tried for ten years to enter that province from the south, and have only just succeeded. It is one of the most anti-foreign provinces in China . . .

Brother, if you would enter that province, you must go forward on your knees." The Goforths took Taylor's advice. They prayed with persistence and gained many prayer supporters back home in Canada. In time, they mastered the language. People began responding to the gospel. A female convert showed outstanding gifts for learning and teaching the scriptures. She became Rosalind Goforth's assistant Bible teacher for women. Years later, in Rosalind's book, How I Know God Answers Prayer, she wrote of miracles of revival, guidance, healing and comfort. Through the Boxer Rebellion and many other life threatening events, the Goforths proceeded on their knees.

Prayer packs a punch. It sends tremors down the enemy's spine. It puts courage in the weak-kneed and takes the whine and worry out of life. It resurrects the fallen and revives the discouraged. Only God can open impenetrable doors. Only He can give us courage to face impossible situations.

His ear is always tilted toward earth, ready to hear our petitions.

"Go forward on your knees" is good advice, not only for missionaries on foreign fields but for ordinary people like you and me. We can face our impossible situations with prayer.

The Simplicity of Prayer

This fight we're in calls for uncomplicated prayer.

Sometimes prayer comes as natural as breathing. I long for time with God, carve slots from my schedule for Him. My prayers soar unhindered like birds in flight. When prayer comes easy, I'll give up anything, even sleep for it. My soul feels deprived if a day passes without prayer.

Prayer fills my spiritual sails with wind and carries me through, and often over, troubled seas. Prayer makes my small contributions to God's kingdom meaningful. It plants holy thoughts in my mind, thoughts higher than those that come to me without prayer. This companionship I feel with Him fills my life with a strong sense of purpose.

But prayer doesn't always come as easily as breathing. I get busy. Lazy. Ignore God. And resist Him. I feel guilty. Then resentful of the guilt. Prayer becomes an up-hill slog. My steps sink in the mire of reluctance. I choose trivial phone calls and even laundry duty over prayer. During these phases, prayer may not come to mind until I flop into bed at the end of the day. If everything you've said about prayer is true, I reason with myself, then why the slog? I must have sinned. I make a mental list of acts I should've done but didn't. Others I shouldn't have but did. Bad attitudes. Thoughtless words. In a short time I've filled an entire page. I proceed down the morbid road of self-examination in search of the particular sin that drove a wedge between God and me. Self-examination is good but, from experience, I know, if carried too far it leads to despair. Self-examination isn't the answer to my dilemma about prayer.

Why shouldn't prayer always come as easy as breathing to people who love God? One day when I wasn't looking for it I found the answer to that question. It appears in Paul's first letter to Timothy. The older apostle is reminding the younger to remain fearless in his faith struggle. Then, he writes the little phrase that caught my attention - "After all, this is a fight we're in." (I Timothy 1:18, The Message)

At fourteen, my pastor's wife asked me– would you like to receive Jesus as your Savior?"

"Yes," I said, not understanding what she meant but knowing it was exactly what I needed. She didn't ask if I wanted to enlist for battle. If she had told me what Paul told Timothy I'd have said, "No thanks, fighting's not my thing. I'm only interested in peace, love and joy."

After decades of loving God, I'm still learning that being a Jesus-follower means doing battle. The obvious opponents – forces that demean scripture and scoff at faith - don't hinder me as much as my tendency to drift into spiritual passivity. Winning this inner battle is more important for my soul's wellbeing than waging war against the latest threat from the New Age or any other movement.

Prayer is needed for the fight we're in. We can't afford to lose our passion for it. One way to revive that passion is to keep prayer simple. Complicated prayer systems creep into the Christian's life. Like weeds they spread roots that choke out the freedom of prayer. Well-meaning speakers urge us to follow their "Ten Easy Steps to Successful Prayer." Before we know it, we're indebted to a system of prayer that soon becomes lifeless. I found a good example of this on one of my bookshelves, a trite little booklet on how to succeed in prayer. It lays out eight points for perfect prayer, each one beginning with the letter P. These helps sound good at first but each person needs to meet with God face to face without a system. It's the only way to get to know Him personally.

Jesus encouraged uncomplicated prayer. "Here's what I want you to do," he said. "Find a quiet, secluded place so you won't be tempted to role-play before God. Just be there as simply and honestly as you can manage. The focus will shift from you to God, and you will begin to sense his grace (Matthew 6:6 The Message)."

Prayer lists can complicate prayer. One of my favourite writers, A. W. Tozer, wrote, "The slave to the file card soon finds that his prayers lose their freedom and become less spontaneous, less effective. He finds himself concerned over whether he did or did not cover his prayer list for the day."[1] Lists take the delight from prayer and turn it into a duty. Simple prayer speaks to God from the heart.

I must accept that when I signed on as a Jesus-follower, I signed up for battle. And that means praying whether I feel like it or not. My sins, though many, haven't caused this battle. It's simply a fact.

When this fight I'm in gets tough and prayer comes hard, I lay aside burdens I've picked up in my journey, burdens that don't belong to me. Like Mary, a close friend of Jesus, I sit at His feet, to listen and adore. In those moments, I know I've not only chosen the best thing, but I'm staying in the fight.

(1) A. W. Tozer, Of God and Men, pp. 79, 81

The Miracle Bus

The most incredible thing about miracles is that they happen.
G. K. Chesteron

Friday night, bone-aching tired from a busy week, I stood with a throng of travelers at the Greyhound Bus depot. It was the beginning of March break and that meant more people than usual were heading out of town. I was going to visit my parents, a three hour journey from our home in Sault Ste. Marie to theirs in Espanola. My father was in the late stages of Alzheimer's disease which meant that he and my mother weren't able to drive to visit my sisters and other relatives. The next day I planned to take them on a road trip.

Standing in the Greyhound parking lot that night my head throbbed as I thought about the next day's road trip. "Lord," I prayed, "save me an alone seat on the bus." I didn't want to share one with a stranger. I wanted to stretch out and relax, maybe even sleep or read the book I carried in my purse. Or maybe lean my head against the window and simply think. That would be nice. Not likely, I thought, too many travelers.

I'm not sure why, but often on buses and planes, strangers sit beside me and unload their sad stories of a chaotic life. When I'm strong, I listen attentively and offer compassion and prayer. But, on that Friday night I wasn't strong. I wanted privacy and quietness. Not sad stories.

One bus pulled into the depot. "Everyone heading to Toronto can board," yelled the attendant. That bus filled quickly and another pulled in. "Every one going to Sudbury and North Bay." The line for this bus seemed endless. When the last person trudged onto it, two people were left standing in the parking lot – a young man who was obviously a student and me. I wondered if they would tell us to go home and come back tomorrow.

A few minutes later a third bus arrived. The attendant gestured for us to board. I headed for the middle section, far enough away from the driver just in case he had a hard luck story to tell. The student disappeared into the dark caverns of the rear seats.

As the bus cruised along Highway 17, I thanked God for answering my impossible prayer. I had only asked that I wouldn't have to share a seat but I had landed a private driver and almost an entire bus to myself. Some must pay a lot for such service but it was included in the price of my ordinary ticket. I scrunched a sweater against the window, leaned my weary head on it and let the gentle jostling of the bus rock me to sleep. At eleven that night Mom met me at the Espanola depot. By then I felt ready to take on the hours of driving that awaited me the next day.

God cares about our basic human needs – like the need for silence and rest. We sometimes fail to ask for these things because we think they're either too small, too impossible or too selfish. We envision God on the fly, juggling the needs of an entire universe, frustrated with the overwhelming task of filling the needs of people more important and more desperate than we are. We need to be reminded that our God is the One who has labeled each hair on our heads with a number. Isn't that a lot more work than reserving a bus for a tired daughter?

The miracle bus reminded me that my needs, all of them, are important to God. Jesus conveyed this message when he said, "You are of greater worth than many (flocks) of sparrows." Luke 12:7

Don't Waste Those Sleepless Nights

Oh those sleepless nights! We stare into the darkness, twist the sheets and re-shape the pillow. We check the clock and moan as time marches toward the alarm. Insomnia makes people do strange things. I read about a woman who cleaned house in the middle of the night. The next day she discovered she'd thrown out many things she should have kept.

Night's wakeful hours make problems seem larger. We worry about things that never cross our minds in the light of day. Sometimes anxious thoughts roar around our minds like an out of control race car. In the morning exhaustion grips body and mind as if we'd never slept at all. What robs us of sleep? Pain, fear, guilt, sorrow, stress are often culprits. Other times, it's nothing we can pinpoint, sleep simply flies away.

Although no one enjoys sleeplessness, night's wakeful hours can be useful. The quiet of darkness is a good time to lift our worries to the Lord in prayer. It's often easier to do this while lying awake in bed because our days are filled with distractions.

King David was acquainted with sleepless nights and wrote of them several times. In Psalm 16:7 he tells how God gave him instruction during the night. The idleness of night gives God an opportunity to drop His thoughts into our minds. Many difficult problems have been solved during a wakeful night. Instead of wasting sleepless hours fuming about tomorrow's fatigue, let's use them to commune with God.

If I'm sleepless at midnight,
I spend the hours in grateful reflection.
Because you've always stood up for me,
I'm free to run and play.
I hold on to you for dear life
and you hold me steady as a post.
Psalm 63:7-8 (The Message)

The World of Words...

No man can be called friendless who
has God and the companionship of
good books.

~Elizabeth Barrett Browning

The Children's Wing

Where I discovered the magic of well-written words.

At ten, I was admitted to the children's wing of a big city hospital. My parents had no choice but to leave me in staff's care and return to our home in a small town an hour away. I shed distraught tears, clung to my mother and begged her not to leave. I watched from my room window as they drove from the parking lot. I was alone in a strange place, without my parents for the first time in my life.

Too old for toys and too young for boys, a tiny library, two shelves at one end of the children's ward play room caught my attention. My fingers rested on The Adventures of Huckleberry Finn. I took the book to my room, climbed up on the bed and opened it. Enveloped by a winter sun that shone through the giant windows lining the outside walls, I allowed Mark Twain to carry me all the way to Mississippi

When evening visiting hours ended, the ward turned into a fairy land of little girls scurrying about in nightgowns with boys in striped old-man pajamas and too-big slippers. Not all patients could scurry. At the end of a central hallway, an iron lung wheezed with the zeal of a vacuum cleaner. It lay on its side like a harmless garbage can but hissed and puffed like a dragon. Inside the dragon, lay a boy my age with polio. I knew about polio. It made my mother and the other mothers in our neighbourhood very nervous. The previous year, two children that we knew had contracted the disease. One lived next door to us.

Although I knew about polio, I didn't know about iron lungs. The two children I knew back home with polio hobbled about on crutches, their legs void of strength. The thought of living every day encased in a metal tube was more than I could fathom. The iron monster was grotesque and frightening. Yet my new friend half-consumed by the dragon seemed content in his universe, and always happy to see us when we scurried to the end of the hall to visit him.

I spent my days with Huckleberry Finn. Twain's vibrant word pictures transported me onto his beloved river and into the lives and language of a people I hadn't known existed. His sentences hummed in my chest, a feeling no other book had given me. In the evenings I joined the scurriers, drawn to the end of the hall by the dragon and the boy caught in its jaws. Childhood empathy in full throttle, we gathered round his head, the only part of him we could see. We chatted, the half-dozen of us, jostling for a position where he could see us without straining his neck.

My stay in this fantasy world lasted a lifetime . . . seven whole days. On the day I left no one warned me my parents were coming to take me home. When they arrived, it took only minutes to pack my things, not enough time to find my hospital friends and say goodbye. Mom and Dad had been pining away at home, worried because they'd left me in tears, with no idea I'd discovered a magical universe and didn't want to hurry away from it. They felt bewildered by my response but kept it to themselves.

Our car, my father's pride and joy, cruised down Highway 17 toward home. I sat in the back seat; my head rested against the side window. For forty miles I sobbed and sniffed. I'd just about got hold of myself when we passed a hitchhiker. Something about a person standing alone on a highway evoked pity in me and tears rolled again. When my parents asked why I was crying, I couldn't answer. I didn't know how to say that I missed the wonderland of the hospital, especially the boy stuck in the dragon's mouth. I missed him most because I knew he'd die. And when he died, there'd be no one to tell me. I didn't even know his last name.

I took the memory of my hospital friends home with me but I never saw or heard from them again. Their names are forgotten, except for one - Mark Twain. I soon bought my own copy of his book and, over time, gave one to everyone who was anyone in my life.

When I walked through our front door, my baby brother's hugs erased my tears. I decided then that Huckleberry Finn must have looked exactly like my brother, Billy, blond curly hair, and a turned-up nose. I rechristened him Huckleberry, Huck for short, and for many years that name stuck.

Today my personal small library lines one wall of my den. On the second from the bottom shelf on the left sits a cluster of books. Their author? My hospital friend, Mark Twain.

Shhh, I'm packing books

We're moving. Today, I'm packing books. "Can't you get rid of some of those books?" my husband asks, not for the first time. He doesn't know that when I move into my new den, I plan to buy more books. *Shhh!*

"Let's make a deal," I say. "You get rid of half of your fishing equipment and I'll get rid of half my books." His tents, sleeping bags and assorted camping stuff fill several shelves in our basement. My book cases neatly line one wall of my study. He walks away.

I'm labeling my boxes by shelf so they'll unpack in the same order. No one knows this yet but I plan to have bigger wall-to-wall shelves in my new den to accommodate more books. It's best not to bring this up right now. *Shhh!*

My husband convinced me to purge my books a few years ago. I thought he might have a point so I did. Just last weekend, Janet Sagle, who has a summer property next door to our little cabin, said she'd picked up a book that had belonged to me from a used book table. "You'd made quite a few notes in it so I thought it must be good," she said. While I contemplated how I could tactfully ask her to return the book, she said she'd passed it on to someone else after reading it. I sighed. It's not easy to say goodbye to books.

I don't coddle my books. Coffee stains, flipped-down pages and post-it notes identify them as mine. Underlines and handwritten notes are precious to me. I seldom part with a book unless it's fiction, and even then, I never part with my favorite mystery novels.

I'm a bit worried about packing my books. We're not moving for two weeks and it could be that I'll need a quote from one or two before then. In the meantime here's a good quote from our old friend Anonymous – If you drop gold and books, pick up the books first, then the gold.

Goodbye – An Inadequate Word

After 31 years, we're moving to a new location so I've been using the word goodbye a lot.

As excited as I am about living in my new home closer to our three children and two grandchildren, saying goodbye has been emotionally draining. Yesterday was my last day at work. I said goodbye to all my co-workers. By evening, I was laying on the couch, energy depleted.

Goodbyes don't come easily for me. I'm struck with dark thoughts like – I'll never see this person again, never engage in conversation with them and I'll never know what happens to them. Yesterday, my co-workers took me out for lunch and showered me with gifts. I feared being swept away by sentimentality. I didn't want to be the weepy mess I was at my graduation. I come from a long line of crybabies and I blame them for the maudlin gene, especially the Irish side of my family.

In my imagination, I hear my close Scottish friend, Ann Laidlaw, saying, "Get a grip on yourself. Of course you won't see most of these people again. We're all dyin' you know. Did you forget that?" Then we'd laugh and she'd remind me of her husband's favorite rendition of goodbye – "Shove off!" Nobody at the office told me to shove off. They dripped kindness all over me. The memory of their hugs clings to my shoulders, a reminder of how blessed I am to have people in my life who make saying goodbye so hard.

Goodbye is a useful word. We use it when we fly out the door to run an errand or to end a telephone conversation. We wave it, blow kisses with it, and even slam doors with it. But there's no getting away from it – some goodbyes are permanent.
Charles Schultz's cartoon character Snoopy summed up my feelings about the word goodbye -

"Why can't we get all the people together in the world that we really like and then just stay together? I guess that wouldn't work.

Someone would leave. Someone always leaves. Then we would have to say goodbye. I hate goodbyes. I know what I need. I need more hellos."

Goodbye is a short form of the phrase, God be with you. That's what I really meant when I said goodbye to my neighbours, co-workers, church friends and hundreds of acquaintances - God be with you.

Nature Speaks

All of creation speaks of the one who spoke it into being . . .

"The heavens declare the glory of God; the skies proclaim the work of his hands. Day after day they pour forth speech; night after night they display knowledge.

There is no speech or language where their voice is not heard.

Their voice goes out into all the earth, their words to the ends of the world." Psalm 19:1-4

Rain

Rain. "Finally," chirps a robin hiding in the maple outside my window. Drops hit the maple's wide leaves, break and splinter into pieces, to the delight of earth. It's been dry. So dry, there's been a province-wide ban on burning. No joking around campfire flames. No poking logs with a stick and watching sparks drift till they disappear.

Today, raindrops kiss the earth with blessings. They kiss on both cheeks. Bless you. Bless you. *Ahhh* sighs the earth, "I thought I'd never see you again." Deep in forested hills on the north side of the city acres of kindling threaten to burst into flame. One spark could ignite hundreds of wooded acres and claim small villages.

Today's rain dampens fire's destructive plans. It seeps through layers of pine needles and leaves into the dry compost beneath. Rain washes dust from trees. They sparkle in green health, as if an ambitious cleaning lady has scrubbed them.

A thirsty earth drinks long and deep. Nature and humanity breathe a relieved sigh. Breezes from open windows blow papers loose from the table top. Welcome winds chase stale odors through screens and deposit fresh smells in every room. Rain is a gift from God.

He bestows rain on the earth; he sends water upon the countryside. Job 5:10

Squeaky Footsteps

When it's many degrees below zero, boots squeak on snow. Breath hangs in the air like little clouds. Noses turn red, frost clings to lashes. A windless frozen day, tree branches sway stiffly, as dangerous as swords.

My feet tramp down the crispy trail; my toes sting with chill. I'm alone in the cold. The sensation links me to nature and it forces me to acknowledge my fragility. Without a warm fire at the end of the trail, my blood would turn to ice; I'd perish. Most days I don't feel my humanity. I don't consider how dependent I am on something as basic as fire. Cold draws out my primitive nature.

Freezing temperatures have medicinal qualities. As a child, our son Carson suffered bouts of croup. My husband and I woke often in the middle of the night to the sound of his whooping gasps. We'd bundle him into a snow suit and carry him outside. While the rest of the street slept, we took turns pacing; back and forth, our steps squeaked on the front porch. Under a dark, star-filled sky, God seemed close. We looked to Him to ease our son's laboured breathing. Step, inhale, step, exhale. Our breath-clouds hung in mid-air.

An hour in the cold. Just what the doctor ordered to open swollen passages. We return our son to his crib. Rest on little one, our squeaky steps have made you well.

Prayer comes easy when accompanied by the sound of my boots squeaking on snow-covered ground. Cold snaps me back to reality; makes me thankful for simple things like fire.

When worry overwhelms, a winter walk can be just what's needed.

Each boot squeak draws us closer to God.

The Maple

From my bedroom window, I looked into the back yard. Overnight winter winds had moved in and dumped a blanket of snow. It lay in clumps on the dead sticks of last summer's perennial garden. It coated the bare branches of our maple tree and made it a stunning sight in white. A designer of hauteur clothing couldn't have done a better job of clothing the tree. "You look lovely this evening. Who are you wearing?" a moderator might ask. "Jack Frost," Maple would reply if he could.

As I watched, a streak of color flitted across the yard toward the tree. Two blue jays perched themselves on separate downy branches. Their arrival seemed planned, as if some magical decorator looked at my maple and said, "Just a hint of colour needed to break the monotony of this pure white scene." The maple came to our yard a few years ago. It had been growing under the deck of our previous house. My husband Doug noticed the spindly, crooked youngster and rescued it. "Any tree trying this hard to survive deserves a chance," he said. In its effort to reach the sun, the maple's thin stem had curved upward between the deck's floor boards. This created a serious weak spot in its trunk. I wasn't too impressed with our new tree and doubted it would last a season. But Doug felt strongly about the maple's possibilities. We tied it to a stake giving special attention to the curve in its spine.

For the first few weeks, we gave the infant tree plenty of water. Winter came and went and the maple survived. When it was three years old, we cut down an aging, messy poplar at the back of the yard. This gave the maple more access to light. Invigorated by our thoughtfulness, its branches soared upward. Now, it's at least thirty feet tall, big enough to provide shade from the sun for our barbecue and seating area. It blesses us every year with a burst of late fall colour. Shade, beauty, a haven for birds – all these benefits come from what once was a skinny sprout that didn't look like it would amount to anything.

Some people, through no fault of their own, get an unfortunate start in life. They try hard and get bent out of shape striving to make something of themselves. It doesn't cost much to support the weak, to lend a helping hand until the person is rooted enough to stand alone, but too few do.

A little verse in Zechariah 4:10 reminds us not to despise the "day of small beginnings." In other words, we shouldn't judge the potential of a person or thing by its early days.

Gladys Aylward, a London parlourmaid believed strongly that God wanted her to go to China. She studied to prepare herself for missionary service but her efforts were not enough. Missionary organizations turned her down. Gladys remained convinced of her calling. She contacted 73 year-old Mrs. Lawson, a woman working alone in a mountainous rural area of China. Through correspondence, Lawson invited Aylward to join her. In 1930 she travelled to China alone at her own expense. When the Japanese invaded, Aylward led scores of refugee children to safety. Her story was told in the movie, *The Inn of the Sixth Happiness*, starring Ingrid Bergman.

By sheer determination, Gladys followed her calling. But it was Mrs. Lawson, a woman able to see potential in a girl of humble means who gave her the opportunity she needed. People, like the maple in my backyard, can break all our predictions about their potential if we give them a little support.

October Lunch Hour

There's a park on the shore of the St. Mary's River, a short walk from my office. When weather permits, and sometimes even when it doesn't, I spend my lunch hours there writing, reading and praying. When staff moves the tables and benches inside for the winter, I'm forced to make other plans. Until then, I get full value from my mid-day breaks by spending them in this naturally refreshing place.

On a late October day I sat at a picnic table in the park surrounded by books, paper and lunch. A north wind sent chills through my too-light sweater while noisy geese congregating nearby, planned their southbound flight. The sun peeked from behind the clouds every few minutes but not long enough to take the shiver from my arms and back.

Others drifted away, driven from the park by the cold. I knew my days there were numbered so I stayed and watched a tour boat make perhaps its last trip downriver. Understanding my sadness at saying goodbye to my lunch hour retreat, a little blast of sunshine blessed me. I wilted with pleasure and thanked God for it.

As I nibbled at my sandwich and let my senses drink in the grandness of my surroundings, from a stand of thick pines came the distinctive whine of bagpipes. After a few priming notes, an invisible piper filled the air with Amazing Grace. Its notes drifted over the water. Quickly tourists gathered on deck, arms wrapped tightly round their trembling bodies. A few walkers broke stride to stand and listen. We didn't speak but we shared a sacred moment on a bleak October day. Tears flowed behind my sunglasses as I remembered the generosity of His grace to me. In my notebook, I wrote -

O limitless grace

Grace that saved my soul from sin

Grace that healed the brokenness within

Grace that brought my loved ones in

Oh Grace, awesome, limitless grace.

Continue strong, continue long

Until that appointed time when all who've

partaken of grace

Will fall in wonder before your face.

RMB

Ten blissful minutes later the phantom piper emerged from nature's closet of pine. We clap, this sprinkling of strangers and me. He takes a bashful bow. *Thank you for warming our souls today by reminding us of God's never-ending kindness.*

Thank you Lord for a glimpse into heaven when I will stand with throngs of people I don't know and together we'll applaud your amazing grace.

Note: The office was Community Living Algoma in Sault Ste. Marie. For many years it was located in the downtown core of Sault Ste. Marie, beside the St. Mary's River.

Look Up

A warm night at the cottage, a camp fire. In rural darkness, the sky shows its glory. Between the tree tops, looking straight up, stars sparkle like crystal, vying for space, nearly bumping into one another.

"Look up," we say to each person as they slide into our circle of lawn chairs. We don't say much else; words to describe the sight above don't exist. We lean back in our canvas slings, fix our eyes upward and let the night sky speak to us.

We view our individual challenges from a higher plane. We allow ourselves to get lost in beauty. We revel in God's handiwork and marvel at His creativity.

Looking up brings relief. Our necessary horizontal view of life requires mundane tasks like paying bills, jockeying for parking spaces, advocating for our children, cleaning and cooking. Simple tasks, but taken together, they exhaust us.

When we look up we let go of the mundane. In letting go, we rest. If only for a few minutes or even an hour, the time we spend looking up renews our ability to handle the trivial but necessary duties that life hands us.

Jesus – a name that connects us to God

And to each other

There is no other name under heaven given among men by and in which we must be saved. Acts 4:12

Late Arrival

These who were hired last worked only one hour, they said, and you have made them equal to us who have borne the burden of the work and the heat of the day. But the landowner answered them, I am not being unfair to you, friend. Didn't you agree to work for a denarius? . . . I want to give the one who was hired last the same as I gave you. (Matthew 20:9-15)

Dad gave to the poor, lived a disciplined life and loved a good joke, but he seemed uninterested in and disconnected from God. In his view, the church persecuted the world by producing endless crops of hypocrites whose religion extended only as far as their wallets. He spoke with some experience. In spite of this strong opinion, he allowed his children to make their own decisions in matters of faith and approved of the family attending church, without him.

For several years after we married and had our own families, my sisters and I fasted and prayed every Monday for Dad. We prayed for a softening in attitude to the gospel and that he would experience a deep sense of need for Christ. Still, whenever the subject of faith came up, Dad recited the long list of rude, money-loving, arrogant hypocrites he'd known. He also knew some godly people but sadly their names never came to his mind. Once, while suffering severe pain in his joints, he welcomed our offer to gather around and pray for him. In minutes, the pain subsided. Several times he stepped close to the brink of believing but he always tripped over the hypocrites.

In his early seventies, our suspicion that Dad had Alzheimer's disease was confirmed. We wondered how long it would be before he lost the ability to understand his need of a Savior. The disease stole Dad's fondest memories and filled him with fear. Like a lost little boy he searched for his parents and older sister. He no longer recognized my mother as his sweetheart but longed for the woman he referred to as his first wife.

My sisters and I left our families to give Mom occasional breaks. While praying the miles away on one of these trips, a heavenly idea came to me – when I arrived, I would take Dad for a walk and I wouldn't return him until I knew he was a believer. A radical plan, but the time had come for a radical idea. After unpacking the car, I said, "Dad, would you like to go for a walk?" His body was strong enough to walk around the world but because he couldn't find his way back, he needed a companion. At the end of the driveway, he slipped his hand in mine. As we walked through autumn leaves, I pointed to a row of maples. "Look at the beautiful colors in those trees, Dad. Jesus made those."

"Uh-huh." His concept of seasons lost, the maples held little interest. His pace slowed as I continued to point. I could almost hear his thoughts,
"There's something new and beautiful."

"Jesus made those for you Dad."

"He did?"

I talked about sky, warmth and wind, mentioning Jesus as the creator of each one, pressing His name into Dad's wounded mind. The longer we talked, the more alert he became.

"Jesus wants you to believe in Him, Dad."

"If I have to be like those people," his voice faltered, "I guess I'll just have to go to hell." It's nothing short of astounding that in his condition he still remembered the hypocrites.

"Jesus doesn't want you to be like them, Dad. He wants you to be like Him."

"He does?"

"Jesus is the only One that matters," I said.

"Jesus," he said slowly, maybe for the first time.

On an almost deserted gravel road, wind tossing leaves at our feet, we said that name together – Jesus. His eyes drifted over my shoulder as he struggled to hold a fleeting thought.

"Jesus," I said to help him stay focused.

"I believe Jesus!" He blurted, voice cracking but determined.

Back at the house, my sister waited in the living room. "Dad, tell Brenda what we talked about on our walk." Most conversations were forgotten within seconds or even mid-sentence.

"I believe Jesus," he said.

From that day until his death a year and a half later, we never doubted the genuineness of Dad's confession.

Jesus told a story about workers hired at different times of the day, some early, some mid-day, others close to quitting time. When payday came, each worker received the same pay. This story illustrates that some people start to follow Christ early in life. Others, like the thief on the cross, make their confession of faith near the brink of death. Yet all receive the same reward. Dad was a late arrival but God will reward him with the same eternal life that all of his followers will receive.

Manitoulin Connections

It's good to know where we come from, what people we belong to and to stay connected to them.

One fall morning, surrounded by empty cottages and bronze maples, I perched on a picnic table at Lake Mindemoya's vacant beach. Quiet waves nudged my thoughts back to childhood memories - swimming for hours with my sisters, sunning ourselves crispy, then years later taking our babies for their first beach experiences. Dad's freshly caught lake trout dinners, Chinese checkers and visits to relatives' homes on rainy days. Memories of these warmed my heart while my body shivered in cool October breezes. It was time to let go of the cottage and that wouldn't be easy.

Nine years a widow, cottage-owner responsibilities had become a burden for Mom. My husband and I had come to the cottage on one last vacation. On arrival, we hammered a For Sale sign into the ground. "It'll go fast," a passerby said. Three bedrooms, attached garage, indoor plumbing, a short sprint to the beach, someone will snatch up your four decades of memories in a hurry.

If not for a small island blocking my view from the picnic table, I would see a hilltop log cabin across the lake. Built by my great-great-grandparents on my mother's side, John and Sarah Galbraith when they were newly married Scottish immigrants, the stone foundations of the cabin are a monument to their determination to carve out a homestead in a new country. They, and other pioneer couples, seeded central Manitoulin Island with their offspring.

My parents, both children of pioneers with farming in their veins, moved to a nearby booming paper town nearby because it promised a better and more regular pay check than life on the farm.

I was four, my sister three when we left what citizens call The Island.

Once a month on Dad's long weekends we made the seventy-mile trip back to Manitoulin to visit grandparents, aunts and cousins. When our family's number reached seven, fitting us into a relative's already full household wasn't easy. So, my parents built the cottage, our Manitoulin home.

When the cottage sells, my identity here disappears. People here know where I come from – "That's Bill and Millie's oldest girl, the folks used to say when I visited the general store near my grandmother's house.

Another would nod, "yea, she's a McCormick alright."

Whenever our toes touched the Island, the local paper added the event to its social column. Even now, mysterious forces report our visits. The following appeared recently - Doug and Rose Brandon and family visited Evelyn Pattison (my aunt) and had lunch with Ted and Georgeanne Legge (my cousins).

Friends who also visit but don't have roots on the Island wonder why our names, and not theirs, appear in print. "You're not connected," I say. My husband's not connected either but he caught onto the importance of connections on his early visits. Other fishermen, recognizing him as a nonlocal, would ask how he knew where to fish. That was another way of asking, "Who are you and where do you come from?" Curiosity is an Island past-time.

His answer was always. "I'm married to Bill McCormick's daughter."
"Is that a fact? That means you're related to the Galbraiths too." He was in, connected, almost as good as home-grown. Son-in-law status became his calling card. Few people know his actual name.

These connections made me reluctant to sell the cottage to strangers. As I gazed at the water, I wondered if I should heed sentimental memories and buy the cottage. Were my memories getting in the way of a common sense decision – letting go.

In the end, I decided that my memories are more than sentiment, that it really matters to me, my children, and their children, that we maintain our connection to Manitoulin Island. We are people who care about treading in the footsteps of our forefathers. I've shown my children John and Sarah's original home. We can envision their tired, scorched bodies dunking in the waters of our lake after a hard day of gathering stones.

That day at the picnic table I decided to buy the cottage. Next summer my first grandchild will be the sixth generation to connect with our Island. I know my pioneer ancestors would be pleased that I've decided to keep my Manitoulin identity.

This piece was published in the first edition of Chicken Soup for the Soul O Canada in 2011.

Reminders

Left untended, life becomes too complicated.

I keep my ideals, because in spite of everything I still believe
that people are really good at heart.

~Anne Frank

One Today is Worth Two Tomorrows

I woke this morning with a list on my brain, things I need to do to get ready to leave for the cottage tomorrow. On top of the list, lay some worries - a suffering friend, bills to pay - and responsibilities - a chapter to write, devotionals due. I pondered these over cereal and coffee . . . then my husband said, "I'm calling Terrence (our grandson) to ask if he wants to come for a morning swim with his Papa." Wet towels . . . ugh, as if there isn't enough laundry? Who wants to swim? I'm busy wondering how I'm going to get everything done today.

Mmm, maybe a swim is what I need. In minutes, our daughter, her husband and two grandchildren were in the pool with us. Two year-old Matilda jumped in without her water wings . . . "lookit me Daddy, I swimming."

We raced from side to side, splashed and talked about the amazing lightning storm last night. Wow! That's the best light show I've seen in years.

We trooped through the kitchen wrapped in wet towels, flipped a few pancakes, cut up cantaloupe and nectarines. Yum. Out came the markers and coloring books. Tension in my shoulders eased.

Our swim party didn't last long but for me it was another decision to live today and let tomorrow worry about itself. Not that I plan to foolishly ignore my responsibilities but I'm trying to approach them from a different direction. A mindset that rolls my worries onto God's big shoulders. . . that's my aim. Choosing to swim with my grandchildren rather than hustle around with worry lines creasing my forehead was good for me. My goal is to live the simple life Jesus advocated –

Give your entire attention to what God is doing right now and don't get worked up about what may or may not happen tomorrow. God will help you deal with whatever hard things come up when the time comes. (Matt. 6:34 The Message)

I must choose to live today and leave tomorrow in God's care because one today is worth two tomorrows.

A Special Gift at Christmas

Joyful little miracles delight the heart.

Shrinking sales had sliced my husband's commission income in half. We trimmed luxury items from the family budget. That meant going without my favorite cologne until business improved. I'd drained the last bottle a few weeks earlier. Christmas season arrived. We earmarked every spare penny for gifts for the kids, food and travel to my parents' home for the holidays. Doug and I decided to forego buying for each other.

A few months before Christmas, Helen began attending our church. I introduced myself and found out she had emigrated from Poland at the end of the Second World War leaving all family members behind. In her sixties, without children, relatives or husband, she filled her days with prayer and Bible reading. Helen sat alone each Sunday, her need for friendship obvious. On the Monday before Christmas, I arranged a luncheon at my home for a few of the older women from church and invited Helen. I intended to introduce her to other Christian women who could become her friends.

When Helen arrived for lunch, she gave me a plate of Christmas baking and a small wrapped package, chocolates I assumed. During our afternoon visit, Helen told the others about her journey to Canada, which included a two-year stopover in Germany. Ilse, another guest, had emigrated from Germany and knew of the camp where Helen had lived. The women listened in wonder as Helen told how she came to know Jesus alone in her bedroom while reading the Bible. Hours flew by without a lull in the conversation. New friendships blossomed.

After my guests left, I quickly prepared a meal for my family. After dinner, clean-up completed, I remembered the little beribboned box from Helen. I opened it expecting to enjoy a delicious chocolate with a relaxing cup of tea.

Instead, I unwrapped a bottle of my favorite fragrance. How could Helen have known? Even my husband who had purchased it several times needed to be reminded of the brand's name.

I phoned to thank Helen for the present. "How did you know that was favorite cologne?" I asked. She told me she'd been shopping in a large department store, walking back and forth among dozens of bottles at the perfume counter. "I simply asked Jesus to show me which one to buy for you," she said. "And He led me to that one."

When we struggle through hard times, it's easy to forget God loves us. He shared a little secret about me with Helen. Her gift of my favorite cologne reminded me not to become discouraged with our financial challenges, God was with us.

Good Things Come in Small Packages

On the last Thursday of November, our town of Caledonia gathered to officially open the Christmas season. We filed out of our homes, down the streets and along the Grand River to The Old Mill. Choirs sang, Winners of a colouring contest were announced. The town mascot led in a countdown – 10, 9, 8 – no sooner had we shouted 1 than a magical light show began. Set to music, lights ran up, down and around the Old Mill. Snow drops lit cedars nearby and running lights outlined a tiny island in the center of the river.

Afterwards my husband and I, with our daughter, her husband and their two children, tramped across the bridge and through the quaint assortment of downtown stores for hot chocolate, apple cider and shortbread. My four-year-old grandson's eyes grew large when he saw rows of Santa cookies in the window of Jones's Bakery, a 100 year plus establishment.

"Is there something in the window you'd like?"

"Gramma, can I have a Santa cookie?"

We opened the ancient door of the bakery and took our places at the end of a line that wound through the store's aisles and ended at the counter. By the time that Santa cookie made it back to the sidewalk, it already had several little bites missing.

I love Christmas but the pressure to buy, buy, buy has stolen some of my joy. I long for simpler ways to celebrate. I experienced one of those simple joys when I saw a little boy grin with delight while he ate a forty-cent cookie. I plan to spend more than forty cents on my grandson's Christmas present but I'm not sure he'll enjoy that gift any more than he enjoyed the Santa face cookie. That reminds of me of a conversation between two fictional but wise characters:

Piglet: The best things come in small packages don't they Pooh?

Pooh: Yes Piglet, very often they do.

Yes, God Really Loves You

At a point in my life when it seemed that my challenges stacked themselves one on top of the other, I struggled to find out why my prayers weren't answered. Had God tired of me? If he had, why? What had I done to offend Him? Many sins came to mind. I confessed them all. Not a bad thing, but it didn't make any difference, trouble kept coming.

During this troubled time, I sought comfort and strength from church. I sat expectantly through worship and preaching but nothing ministered to my soul. One night I returned home from service utterly desperate. I went into our bedroom, left the lights off, sank to my knees by the bed and prayed. I planned to stay until the Lord spoke to me but after an hour I rose from my knees with the same sense of soul desperation.

In that desperate moment, while standing at the window facing our dark back yard, I made this decision: I'd already committed my life to Jesus and I wouldn't turn back, no matter what. That decision led to a declaration that went something like this: Lord, if you never answer another prayer for me as long as I live, I'll still serve you. What you've done for me already is far more than I expected when you and I began our journey together. If I live the rest of my life in this dark pit, then so be it; I'll keep my pledge to you anyway.

What difference did that decision make? My faith became rooted in Christ, in Him only, and not in circumstances. His love for me is always the same, enormous, in good times and bad. Troubles come to everyone and I am no exception. Troubles still come but my perception of them has changed.

Facing challenges on several fronts? Perhaps your sufferings have caused you to question whether God really loves you. *HE DOES*. His unconditional love for you never waivers. You can depend on it today, tomorrow and forever.

Let these words from Paul sink into your soul today.

"For I am persuaded beyond doubt – am sure – that neither death, nor life, nor angels, nor principalities, nor things impending and threatening, nor things to come, nor powers, nor height, nor depth, nor anything else in all creation will be able to separate us from the love of God which is in Christ Jesus our Lord." Romans 8:38,39 (AMP)

Don't Underestimate God

Of the twelve spies who went into the Promised Land, ten brought back a godless report. They exaggerated the size and power of the inhabitant tribes. Only two men returned to the Israelite camp with a good report – Joshua and Caleb. They said, "Let's go up and take the country. It's a good land and we're strong enough to take it."

The Israelites looked at numbers. Ten against, two for. Then they chose to shake in their boots with the fearful ten. That choice led to a lot of whining and complaining. Some even made plans to return to lives of slavery in Egypt.

The Israelites did what we often do. They overestimated the power of evil and underestimated the power of God. They accepted bad news as fact. Often information from experts turns out to be tainted by pre-conceived ideas, faulty input or personal agendas. In the 1970s a movie circulated amongst many evangelical churches. It showed maps of the world illustrating how Communism would eventually take over the whole world – doom, doom, doom.

Like the enemy tribes of Israel, Communism had many weak spots. It wasn't invincible. Their takeover of the world wasn't imminent. God was at work behind the scenes taking it apart brick by brick until it tumbled, seemingly overnight.

Many of the challenges we face today appear impenetrable. They make scary noises, spread false rumors of destruction. If we believe the stories of doom, we will fall into the same trap the Israelites fell into – the trap of disrespecting God.

We must always be careful not to overestimate the power of evil and thereby underestimate God's power to destroy evil. If we view the world as a great enemy, able to take us down at any moment, we will end up living a faithless fearful life.

Forty years later, the quivering voices of the fearful Israelites were dead. Joshua and Caleb, men of faith and courage took charge and led the
Israelites to victory.

Will you side with the fearful ten or the faithful two?

Lord, I'm tired of living in fear. I choose to accept the courage you offer me. I pledge to take care not to underestimate your power to change any situation.

Stand Alone Words

Some words are so vital they stand

up straight without the aid of other

words.

Here are a few straight standing words.

Persistence

So I say to you, ask and keep on asking and it shall be given you; seek and keep on seeking and you shall find; knock and keep on knocking and the door shall be opened to you. For everyone who asks and keeps on asking receives; and he who seeks and keeps on seeking finds; and to him who knocks and keeps on knocking, the door shall be opened. Luke 11:9,10 (AMP)

Persistence is important in all areas of life but nowhere more important than in prayer. Jesus told of a man who knocked at his friend's door late at night. He needed bread to feed a late visitor. The friend tucked in for the night refused to get up. The man knocking wouldn't to take "no" for an answer. It was his "keep on knocking" characteristic that caused the sleepy man to get out of bed and give his neighbor bread.

In Barnes' commentary, he writes, "If the thing (we ask for) is for our good, and if it is proper that it should be granted . . . let us inquire whether God has promised such a blessing, and then let us persevere (in prayer) until God gives it."

Too often we pray a few times for a promised blessing and then give up. After praying for the infilling of the Spirit a few times, a man concluded, "Well, God knows where I live and if He wants to fill me with His Spirit, I'm available." If our employer forgot to pay us, would we not make phone calls and visit his office continually until he cut us a check? We wouldn't leave money that rightfully belonged to us unclaimed.

Jesus, the giver of many unclaimed gifts, has planned to give them to the persevering. Are you continually knocking and asking for God's good things – salvation for loved ones, the power of the Holy Spirit, guidance, wisdom, opportunities to witness, employment and so much more – if you are, keep on. If you've given up in despair, grab the doorknocker of Heaven again.

Nothing in the world can take the place of persistence
Talent will not –

Nothing is more common than unsuccessful men with talent

Genius will not –

Unrewarded genius is frequently found
Education will not –

The world is full of educated derelicts.

Persistence alone is unbeatable.

Lord, thanks for the reminder to persist in asking for your blessings. My fingers are ever knocking at your door.

Hosanna

Hosanna! One of my favorite words, a celebration word, it exalts God to the highest heaven. When "thank-you Lord" and "praise God" seem weak and unsatisfactory, we can dig deep and find that perfect word - Hosanna.

The crowds who hailed Jesus as the long-promised Messiah and led His procession into Jerusalem one week before the crucifixion used that word - Hosanna. They had watched Him relieve the afflicted of demons. Their hearts had burned within them as they listened to His teaching. They said, "No man has ever taught like this man."

When the crowds saw Jesus set the afflicted free, joy overcame them. They spread their cloaks on the ground, a carpet for Him. They sliced branches, laid them on the road to cushion his ride. They danced, sang and shouted, "Hosanna!"

According to Strong's Exhaustive Concordance (a book thick enough to stand on to reach a high cupboard), Hosanna is used only six times in the Bible - three times by Matthew, twice by Mark and once by John. All three were disciples of Jesus.

Hosanna is a marvelous word. I wish we used it more often. It stirs the Spirit. It's a word perfectly suited to Jesus and to no one else. Besides being a praise word, it can also mean save us. Jesus, the One and only Savior earned our Hosanna praise by His death on the cross and His resurrection from the dead.

As we remember Christ's death and resurrection, let's remember the word Hosanna - praise and exalt Jesus for giving His life to save us from our sins.

"Hosanna in the highest!"

Unspoken

I'm sometimes too quick to express my mind. I hate to admit it – but I get cranky. And cranky isn't good. Remember who you are, I remind myself – an ambassador for Christ. And there's nothing He needs less than a cranky representative. James, leader of the early church, wrote, ". . . the tongue is as dangerous as any fire, with vast potentialities for evil. It can poison the whole body, it can make the whole of life a blazing hell." James 3:6 (J.B. Phillips)

When the Holy Spirit arrived, He announced His coming with wind that blasted through a meeting room where 120 Christ-followers waited and prayed. Flames of fire spread around the room, resting on each of them. And then, the Spirit gave every man, woman and child present the ability to speak in a language they'd never known.

The Spirit showed at His coming on the Day of Pentecost that He wants control of our tongues. This includes not only our words but our expression of them because people hear not only what we say but how we say it. A Christian woman in the community visited our home often. She loved the Lord but her reputation as a professional griper suited her. One day one of my young sons asked, "Why is that lady always angry?" A complaining tone colored every word that came out of her mouth. Even her prayer requests sounded like an accusation against God for not yet sending an answer. This woman prayed continually for her family's salvation but sadly, her untamed tongue continues to drive them away from God.

The Christian's unrestrained tongue is an enemy within the church that destroys more of God's work than enemy devices from outside. Many sins lurk on the tongue – gossiping, slandering, lying, rudeness and even crankiness. "No one can tame the human tongue," James says. (James 3:8)

What can I do then?

Am I doomed to repeatedly disappoint God and myself by speaking in a way that dishonors Him?

Help comes from Paul. "I urge you, in view of God's mercy, to offer your bodies as living sacrifices, holy and pleasing to God – this is your spiritual act of worship." Romans 12:1 (NIV)

The Spirit urges us to lay our complete selves, including our tongues, on God's altar. He asks us to leave hurtful words and griping thoughts unspoken.

Prayer: Lord, as an act of worship, I dedicate my whole being to you. May good and not evil come from my lips today. Holy Spirit, keep me aware of how my words affect others.

Transitions

My daughter teared up when her husband dismantled the crib. Their youngest turned three a couple of days ago and she has tired of her baby bed and wants a big girl bed to replace it. So down came the crib and up went a big girl bed. Goodbye to babyhood.

Transitions. Life is filled with them. Some bring tears, others laughter but all mean saying goodbye. Retirement means goodbye to work-life, a welcome transition in some ways but not in all ways. A new home, different job, graduation, marriage, divorce, birth, death - change is inescapable.

Even joyful transitions can leave us a little dazed. Walking away from the past, even a painful one, means adapting to change. Victims in transition have to be willing to give up a macabre attachment to gloom. We might think that would be easy but letting go of emotional pain means becoming someone new, building better attachments and being willing to lay down anger and revenge. That's a challenge.

Life pushes us from one phase to another. It doesn't wait for us to wet our toes in the future before deciding to plunge. Often it heaves us off the end of the dock into deep water - sink or swim it says.

With God's help we can embrace the future with hope. We can say goodbye to cribs, open the door of independence for children, move our belongings across the country and take up residence in new neighbourhoods, retire from our jobs and take on new projects. We can do it because God is with us, urging us to discover joy in each new phase of life.

Are you in transition? Moving from a comfortable stage of life to an awkward one? I find it helps to remember past changes and how we survived them. It bolsters our courage for new challenges. Psychologist, Norman H. Wright, makes a good suggestion - write a goodbye letter to the past. Putting our feelings to paper is therapeutic. We often find comfort in our own words.

As someone once said - the best sermons we'll ever hear are the ones we preach to ourselves.

Your eyes saw my unformed substance,

and in Your book all the days of my life

were written before ever they took

shape,

when as yet there was none of them.

(Psalm 139:16 AMP)

He is Emmanuel, God with us, with us before any of our features were formed, with us before our first transition was made . . . and with us when we make life's final transition into the arms of Jesus.

Lord, help me to accept the changes that each phase of my life brings. I know you are with me, helping me to find good in all situations and using all circumstances in my life to draw me closer to you.

Transformation

At 14, I was a disgruntled church-goer. I went because it was one of Mom's compulsories. As young as 5, I couldn't wait for Sunday School to end. By the time I was a teenager my dislike for church was in full throttle. I sat with ears closed impatient for the benediction.

Two months before my fifteenth birthday, a young couple came to pastor our shabby little church. (The people weren't shabby, only the building.) My cousin, who loved church almost as much as I hated it, asked me to go to a Sunday evening service, something I'd never done. Since we were joined at the hip, I went. The sermon went in one ear and out the other. Afterwards, the pastor invited the congregation to join him in the prayer room. Everyone filed out of the pews and downstairs to a squat little room with wooden benches. I went because not going would've drawn attention to myself.

On my knees at a bench, the pastor's wife, a 22 year-old newly-wed, came and knelt beside me. Her name was Bev Friesen. She whispered, "Would you like to receive Jesus Christ as your Savior?"

I said, "Yes" because I knew it was the right answer. I repeated after her a simple prayer. The meeting soon ended and I went home. When I opened my eyes the next morning, something stirred in my chest. I felt new inside, as if I was breathing different air than I had the day before. On the way to school, everything around me seemed re-born - sky, grass, sounds. Over the next few days, people I hadn't much cared for became loveable. I'd stepped into a fresh world.

My attitude toward church changed. I, who had no use for Sunday School, became a diligent teacher of a young class. By praying a simple prayer to receive Jesus as my Savior, I experienced a spiritual birth.

One night a rabbi, Nicodemus, came secretly to Jesus to ask what he thought were deep questions. Jesus answered him, "You must be born again." A simple answer for a scholar who didn't want his colleagues to see him conversing with Jesus.

Nicodemus remembered Jesus' words. After the crucifixion, he became a daylight disciple. Along with Joseph of Arimathea, another night follower, he went to Pilate and requested Jesus' body. They lovingly wrapped it and laid it in a new tomb. Like me, Nicodemus was born again.

This Easter, as I ponder my youthful transformation, I still feel awed by Jesus, still see the world through His eyes. Two thousand years after his death and resurection, Jesus is still birthing people into His kingdom. Have you experienced spiritual birth?

The young pastor's wife led me in a prayer that went something like this:

Lord Jesus, I believe you are the Savior of the whole world and that no one can experience spiritual birth except through you. I invite you into my life today and give you permission to erase my sin and transform me.

A Final Word

When all the words have been spoken and written that will be spoken and written the only words that will remain are God's words and the words He speaks through us.

Keep His words close to your heart so that your heart and mind will be full of His words.

Keep telling your God story. Through your story people will see that God's words transform lives.

Keep on living for Him because God's active words are visible through your kind acts and good deeds.

Keep on praying because prayer takes ordinary words, launches them into the heavens where they are weaponized and then dispatches them back to the earth where they become emissaries that accomplish His will.

Watch your words. Are there words that should be eliminated from your vocabulary? Words that curse, boast, whine, lie, deceive, cause dissension and hurt feelings, these have no place on the tongues of people whose hearts are tied to God's heart.

The Servant of God says the Lord God has given me the tongue of a disciple and of one who is taught, that I should know how to speak a word in season to him who is weary.

(Isaiah 50:4 AMP)

Other Books by Rose McCormick Brandon

Promises of Home – Stories of Canada's British Home Children

He Loves Me Not, He Loves Me

Vanished – What Happened to my Son?

Contact Rose McCormick Brandon at
rosembrandon@yahoo.ca

Visit the author's website, Writing from the Heart, at

http://writingfromtheheart.webs.com

One Good Word Makes all the Difference

A good word at the right time, whether spoken or written, gives hope to the discouraged and comfort to the broken-hearted. Good words inspire us to follow in the footsteps of God and give us courage to remain faithful to Him. They heal our wounds and warm our souls. Long after we've forgotten the source of encouraging words, their influence remains because good words make themselves at home in our hearts for a lifetime.

ROSE MCCORMICK BRANDON

ROSE MCCORMICK BRANDON's award-winning work has been published in more than twenty-five publications. She is the author of three other books - Promises of Home – Stories of Canada's British Home Children, He Loves Me Not He Loves Me and Vanished - and dozens of articles. A member of The Word Guild and The Manitoulin Writers Circle, Rose publishes two blogs: Listening to my Hair Grow (faith writings) and Promises of Home (stories of child immigrants).

Rose and husband, Douglas, summer on Manitoulin Island where her pioneer ancestors settled and the home of his favourite fishing holes. The rest of the year, they live in Caledonia, Ontario. near their three children and two grandchildren.

$15.00

ISBN 978-0-9780622-4-8
61500
9 780978 062248

writingfromtheheart.webs.com
rosemccormickbrandon.wordpress.com